Acknowledgment:

I want to express my heartfelt gratitude to my wife, my children, my church family, my coworkers, and all the wonderful people who have shared my life and contributed to the creation of this book.

Introduction

I wrote this book with two primary intentions. First, I wanted to document my life's journey—capturing the lessons learned, pivotal experiences, and values that have shaped me. By doing so, I aim to leave a meaningful legacy for future generations, offering them insights gained from decades of triumphs, failures, and growth. This book is not merely a reflection of my path but an invitation to explore the enduring truths that connect us as human beings navigating life's complexities.

While my achievements may appear admirable, it is often my failures and disappointments that hold the most valuable lessons. These struggles have been my greatest teachers, revealing insights that success alone could never provide.

My second intention is to inspire others to reach their fullest potential. As a lifelong teacher and mentor, I am passionate about education and motivation. Through this book, I aim to share the knowledge and wisdom I've gained to empower others.

On a personal level, writing this book has been an extraordinary and transformative journey. It has fostered growth, brought clarity, and renewed my sense of direction. Reflecting on moments of joy, pain, and discovery has been profoundly therapeutic, helping me process emotions, uncover fresh perspectives, and strengthen my sense of purpose. This journey has illuminated the deeper meaning of perseverance, adaptability, and thriving in adversity—qualities I hope to instill in my readers.

Ultimately, this book serves as both a mirror and a guide—a mirror reflecting my own evolution and a guide for others on their unique journeys. My hope is that by sharing my story, I can contribute to the lives of others, encouraging them to embrace their potential, learn from their struggles, and move forward with renewed strength and determination.

Contents

1.   Matric

I transferred from Tafari Makonnen School to Prince Makonnen High School. Prince Makonnen was a better fit for me; it was closer to home. Over time, I found my footing, and I became more motivated to study hard. Out of 250 students in the 9th grade, I ranked 35th. I was elated, but when I showed my great-grandmother my results, she didn't understand why I was so excited since I wasn't ranked first or second. But for me, it was a great accomplishment.

When we were promoted to the 10th grade, they gathered all the top students from eight 9th grade sections and placed us in one class. In the 9th grade, I was competing with the entire student body, but in 10th grade I was in a class with the smartest students and the competition got tougher. I barely passed the class that year. However, things changed in 11th grade when we had a Peace Corps volunteer who taught us math. His teaching method was exactly what I needed to understand the subject. I did my homework daily, which helped me develop good study habits. He motivated me to stay focused on my education. He was the reason that I was able to major in STEM when I went to the university.

In 12th grade, the second semester was dedicated to preparing for the 12th-grade exam, which we called the matric exam. I felt completely lost and unsure of what to study. During a visit to my uncle, he asked me what I was studying and what textbooks I had. I didn't have any textbooks or study materials, nor did I have any practice questions. My uncle gave me previous years' exams to practice with. Around the same time, I befriended a classmate who had consistently been top of his class since the first grade. I asked if I could study with him; he invited me to stay at his house for three weeks before the exam. I observed how he studied; he used multiple books for one subject and worked on problems even before the teacher had lectured on them. We studied together, and soon it was time to take the matriculation exam.

When the results were finally posted at the school gate, I made my way there with great anticipation, knowing that this moment would determine the course of my future. The matriculation exam was a pivotal milestone for every student. If I passed, I would be eligible to attend university with all expenses paid, an opportunity that was not just a personal achievement but a life-changing privilege. However, if I failed, the path ahead would be much harder. I would have to attend night school, retake the exam, and delay any hopes of pursuing higher education.

As I walked toward the gate, the tension within me grew. The future of my dreams—everything I had worked for—seemed to hang in the balance. I knew that passing would not only open the doors to university but would also bring honor to my family and prove to myself that all the effort and sleepless nights had been worth it. Failure, on the other hand, felt like an immense weight that could crush my aspirations.

As I neared the crowd of students gathered around the gate, I heard my name being called. Several classmates began congratulating me, and for a moment, I didn't fully understand what was happening. Was it possible that I had passed? I pushed through the crowd, heart racing, trying to see for myself. My hands were trembling as I scanned the list of names, and then I found it—my name was there! I had passed!

Out of 250 students, only nine had succeeded, and I was one of them. In that moment, a rush of emotions overwhelmed me. Relief, pride, joy—everything came flooding in at once. I had never dared to imagine, even in my wildest dreams, that I would be among the few who passed. The reality that I would now be able to attend university—something that had once seemed like an unreachable goal—was astonishing. It felt unreal, almost as though I was standing outside myself, watching this extraordinary moment unfold. Our graduation was held in a grand hall; I had the honor of shaking hands with Emperor Haile Selassie as I received my diploma. It was one of the proudest moments of my life! I had proven to myself and others that I could pass matriculation and could pursue a college education.

Be kind to everyone you meet, for they may be facing battles you know nothing about.

2. Life Lessons from the Kitchen to the Dumpster

When I first arrived in this country, I was hired as a dishwasher at an Italian restaurant on 17th Street in Washington, DC, earning fourteen dollars a day. The kitchen was always busy, especially during breakfast and lunch, and the chefs would finish cooking and toss their pots and pans into the sink, causing the dishes to pile up high. My friend, who worked alongside me, had a different approach; he would fill the sink with hot, soapy water, drop the pots in to soak, and then casually sit down with his newspaper, allowing the grease to loosen for easier cleaning. I, however, lacked the patience for that—I felt uncomfortable watching the pile grow, so I would grab a scrubber, roll up my sleeves, and scrub the grime away until the pots were clean. When I finished scrubbing the last pan, my friend would calmly fold up his newspaper and effortlessly finish his share, while I had already worked through the toughest part.

Looking back, I see how this job set the tone for much of my life. Fast forward 50 years, and this week, I found myself needing to dispose of some old furniture—a loveseat, a sofa, and a few other pieces. I planned to haul them to the dumpster myself, but it wasn't as simple as I thought. The glass cabinet was easy; I separated the top from the bottom, loaded it into my van, and drove it to the dumpster. The recliner sofa, however, was bulky, heavy, and awkward to handle. Just when I was about to give up, my neighbor unexpectedly came over to help. Together, we lifted it into the van, and when I arrived at the dumpster, a lady asked if I needed help. She then asked me to stand by as she single-handedly carried both pieces to the dump.

The real challenge came with the loveseat. It took me over two hours to break it apart, and I had to be strategic about it, carefully dismantling the armrests, backseat, and metal frame to fit everything into my van. The metal frame was the heaviest part, but with a handcart, I was able to maneuver it. When I arrived at the dumpster, someone else helped me unload it. Somehow, I always seem to get help at the right moment, just when I need it the most.

Here's a simple lesson I've learned: sometimes, to move forward, we need to take things apart first. Just like I had to break down the loveseat to make it fit, life often requires letting go of old habits or ideas to make space for new ones. Understanding that both building and breaking down are part of growth is important. While being independent and doing things on our own is valuable, we shouldn't hesitate to accept help when it's offered. I realized I didn't have to do everything by myself. Lastly, I need to be mindful of my impatience; while quick action can be good, sometimes waiting or finding an easier way can save us effort. Hard work, self-reliance, and knowing when to accept help are all crucial in navigating life's challenges.

By nature, we are problem solvers.

3. <u>Education</u>

When I first came to this country, I was determined to change my life! As a first-generation migrant, I quickly realized that achieving success often required being born into a wealthy family, marrying into wealth, starting a business, or pursuing an education. I chose to pursue education. I applied to American University, Georgetown University, George Washington University, Catholic University, and Howard University, but received rejection letters from these prestigious institutions.

Unswervingly, I drew a circle representing a one-hour driving distance around Washington, D.C. and applied to colleges and universities within that area. Eventually, a small college in Baltimore, known today as Coppin State University, accepted me. I was elated. Within six months of my arrival in the U.S., I packed my belongings and moved to Baltimore. Thanks to the credits I had earned in Ethiopia, I was able to complete my degree in chemistry in just two and a half years!

When I began applying to graduate schools, I was surprised to be accepted into Howard University's graduate program, despite having been rejected by them for undergraduate studies. At Coppin State, the university lacked the facilities for proper laboratory work, and my professors could only demonstrate a few experiments. As a result, I graduated with a bachelor's in chemistry without knowing the difference between a test tube and a beaker!

Howard University was a different world. The chemistry majors there had taken intensive courses in general, organic, analytical, and physical chemistry, both in lecture and laboratory settings, making them fully qualified graduate students. Some had even earned master's degrees from prestigious institutions like MIT and from universities in India. I, on the other hand, was completely unprepared for graduate school. The chairman of the chemistry department offered me a full scholarship on the condition that I earned a B in all my classes. As a proud graduate of Coppin State, I naively thought achieving three B letter grades would be easy. However, I soon found myself working tirelessly to meet this goal.

At the end of the semester, I was relieved to have passed all three of my courses with a B letter grade. With a three-hundred-dollar stipend every two weeks and free tuition, I was able to complete my education. During my time at Howard, I co-authored two research papers with my research advisor, which qualified me for my Ph.D. I completed my degree in four years, becoming the first among my classmates to earn a Ph.D.

When I began job hunting, I found an opening at Georgetown University. Ironically, the institution that had once rejected me as a student now hired me with a salary of over $30,000. Looking back, I've learned some important lessons. First, perseverance is key! Even after facing many rejections, I didn't give up. Instead, I kept trying and eventually found a way forward, realizing that setbacks are just chances to rethink and keep moving toward your goals.

Second, adaptability is important. Moving to Baltimore and attending Coppin State University taught me to adjust to new situations and make the best of what I had. I also learned the importance of preparation. At Howard University, I struggled because I wasn't fully ready for the challenges, but through hard work, I overcame those obstacles. Lastly, life is full of surprises! Even though Georgetown University once rejected me, it became the place where I started my career.

Iron only softens when it melts.

4. Exercise

Exercise has become an essential part of my life, but it wasn't always that way. In fact, I didn't seriously start exercising until I was in graduate school. My best friend at the time had high blood pressure, and his doctor advised him to run every day to help manage it. Knowing I wasn't very active, he would invite me to run with him, even going so far as to bribe me with dinner or offering me a ride home. He did everything he could to motivate me because at the age of 24 he saw the need for me to take better care of my health. At that point, I was about 20 pounds overweight, and I knew I needed to make some changes.

The first step for me was losing that extra weight. I committed myself to a strict diet and some in-house exercises. For two months, I stuck to a regimen of eating mainly steak and salad, avoiding foods that would hinder my progress. Slowly but surely, the pounds started to come off, and by the end of those two months, I had shed the extra weight. The difference in how I felt was incredible—I was lighter, more energetic, and more capable of taking on physical activity. It was then that I finally felt ready to embrace running and exercise.

With my friend's ongoing support and encouragement, I made exercise a regular part of my routine. We used to go to Anacostia Park together, running about 3 ½ miles in just half an hour. It wasn't easy at first, but I stuck with it, and over time, I grew to enjoy it. We kept this up for a solid six years, all while I continued to play tennis, another activity I enjoyed. Looking back, those years of commitment to exercise not only helped me stay fit, but they also built a foundation for healthy habits that would last a lifetime.

After those six years, even as life got busier and circumstances changed, I continued to prioritize exercise. Whether it was by joining a gym or making a habit of walking every morning, I found ways to keep moving and stay active. Now, at 75 years old, I've adjusted my routine to suit my body's needs, but I'm proud to say that exercise is still a central part of my life. These days, I go to water aerobics three times a week, which is great for low-impact movement, and I also make sure to walk for at least half an hour every morning. This combination of exercise keeps me feeling healthy, mobile, and energized as I continue to age.

The neck that fails to carry the head is like a foundation that cannot support the structure.

5. Rejection

Rejection is a part of life, and it happens to everyone in many ways. It's the feeling we experience when we are not wanted, appreciated, or valued—when we are tossed aside as if we are no good. Statistics show that everyone faces rejection at least seven times in their lifetime, with every pastor experiencing seven rejections in a year. Even children whose earliest memories are around three or four years old, encounter rejection they may remember for life.

Children experience rejection in various situations: when they are not chosen to play on a sports team, when they raise their hands to answer, but the teacher never calls on them, when parents favor others, when they are compared to other children, and when friends reject them. As they grow older, they will face even more forms of rejection. So, why not learn from the Master, Jesus Christ, who was rejected in His hometown? In the Gospel of Luke, chapter 4, verse 28, Jesus was in the synagogue reading from the book of Isaiah, yet the people rejected Him. They even tried to throw Him off a cliff. The scribes rejected Him as well, disliking how He healed on the Sabbath and disregarding their additional rules beyond scripture. The people in the synagogue were furious when they heard His parables, driving Him out of town and taking Him to the brow of the hill on which the town was built to throw Him off the cliff. But we read that He walked right through the crowd and went on His way.

Looking back on my life, I've also experienced rejection. While working at the Naval Research Lab, after one contract was finished, I applied for jobs at ninety-two different places and was rejected by all of them. Yet, the job waiting for me was in the same building, on the same floor, right across from where I was already working. I also faced rejection when I performed several experiments, and my boss, along with his superior, wrote up the results and applied for a patent, leaving my name out. This marked the beginning of my journey to North Carolina. Even though the experience was painful, there was a different plan for my destiny. Throughout my chemistry career, I've applied for grants, raises, and promotions, only to be met with rejections.

So, what has helped me overcome rejection? First, I know it's a part of life. I'm not the only one experiencing it—everyone does. I view rejection as evidence that I'm doing something creative. Some people will like it, and some won't. But one thing I've always done is keep moving. The Bible tells us that Paul was rejected by the Jews, which led him to preach to the Gentiles—a major accomplishment and the start of a lifelong ministry. In the book of Acts, we read that Paul rejected John Mark, believing he wasn't fit for ministry. But what did John Mark do? He kept ministering and eventually reconciled with Paul, later going on to write the Gospel of Mark. When people do not value us, we should keep going. The lesson is to never give up! When I feel left out, I keep trying. When I feel like no one wants me around, I keep believing in myself. When others don't see my value, I remain strong. I keep moving forward until I reach my goal because my mission is bigger than my rejection!

When I was single, my mother suggested an arranged marriage for me, and I was on my way to Nairobi to meet my future wife for the first time. I had been excited for months, imagining what it would be like to finally see her after so many phone calls and messages. When I stood in front of her, my heart raced with nervousness. If she didn't like me, it would have been heartbreaking. The thought of being rejected after coming so far would have been painful and embarrassing. I wasn't sure what I would do. I wanted to cry but tried to stay strong, even though I felt frozen with fear. Running away wasn't something I would do, but rejection would have hurt me deeply, making me feel unworthy. If she had turned me down, I would have quietly left, holding back my tears until I got into a taxi, where I would have broken down, mourning the future I thought we'd have. Thankfully, she didn't reject me and accepted me as her future husband.

A jeep carries us to the battlefield, but it won't fight our battles.

6. Children Home Care Center

I was recently invited to an Ethiopian New Year
celebration by one of my daughters, which brought back
memories of how I first became involved with a children's
home care center. It all began while I was reading George
Muller's best-selling book Releasing the Power of Prayer. I
was deeply inspired by his unwavering faith and wanted to
experience the effectiveness of prayer myself. At the time, I
was unemployed, and my youngest sister had invited me to
her wedding. My wife, Tenu, was pregnant with our
daughter, and thankfully, my other sister was available to
help look after her while I traveled to Ethiopia for the
wedding.

While celebrating with my family, I became acutely
aware of the need for children's services, especially in the
wake of the Ethiopian famine. During that time, countless
families had fled to feeding camps throughout the country
in search of survival. However, once the crisis passed and
families returned to their homes, they left behind 250,000
children in those camps, with no one to care for them. The
government was at a loss, unable to provide resources or
figure out how to manage the overwhelming number of
abandoned children.

Amid the wedding festivities, I also found time to visit
the Children's Commission to explore ways I could help.
With no job and limited financial means, I returned to the
United States, determined to find a way to make a
difference. On my next trip to Ethiopia, I signed an
agreement with the Children's Commission, starting with

four children. I hired a housemother and a cook to look after them. By this time, my family had settled in Raleigh, and I had found work as a chemistry teacher. Each time I visited Ethiopia, I accepted four more children, eventually bringing the total to seventeen.

The support I received was minimal, but I was able to supplement it with my income and donations. I established a 501(c)(3) nonprofit and began accepting contributions, which helped keep the home running. However, running the children's home was not without its challenges. Employee issues and visa complications were constant hurdles. One of the major problems I faced was with immigration. There was another man with the same name as mine who had committed serious crimes, which led to constant confusion. Every time I traveled in and out of the country, I was detained for hours—sometimes up to four—while authorities investigated my identity. This was not only frustrating for me but also for the people who came to pick me up from the airport.

Thankfully, my late cousin worked in airport customs and often helped me get through immigration more smoothly. However, the final obstacle came in 2008 when I was detained for so long that I wasn't allowed to enter the country. That experience made me question whether I was still needed in that role and whether I should continue forcing myself on a country that seemed to put up so many barriers.

At that point, I decided my efforts would be better spent helping people in the United States—the country that had welcomed me and allowed me to grow and serve. With the help of my youngest sister, I began the process of closing the orphanage. Most of the children had grown up and completed college, and my sister was able to find care for the few who remained. After 15 years of service and raising seventeen children, I made the difficult decision to close the children's home care center, knowing that it had made a lasting impact on the lives of those it touched.

7. Deeper Than I Thought

When I was working at the dollar store that Tenu and I
owned, I developed a wound on my thumb that simply
wouldn't heal. Every time I used the cash register to punch
in numbers, the wound would throb with pain, and it
seemed like no matter what I did, the healing process was
stalled. I tried using band-aids to protect it, but that didn't
seem to help either. Eventually, I decided to leave it
uncovered, thinking that maybe exposing it to air might
help the healing. I even tried using medical tape to cover it
when it got too painful, but nothing was working. The
wound was small, but it was causing me a lot of discomfort,
and I didn't know what else to do.

One day, the leaders of my church came to visit me at
my house. During their visit, I asked them if they would
pray for my thumb, as the pain was becoming unbearable,
and I was desperate for healing. To my surprise, after their
prayer, the wound finally started to heal. It was a miracle—
the pain subsided, and soon after, my thumb was back to
normal. From that point on, it never bothered me again. I
was so relieved and thankful for their prayers.

However, a few months later, something else happened
that made me realize the problem was deeper than I initially
thought. I was driving to Washington, DC, when I noticed
that my mouth was constantly dry, and I had to urinate
frequently. It was a strange feeling, one that I had never
experienced before. Concerned, I called my brother and
explained my symptoms to him. He immediately suspected
that I might have diabetes and suggested we check my

blood sugar. When he tested my glucose levels, they were so high that they exceeded the limit of his testing instrument, which only measured up to 600 milligrams per deciliter. I was shocked!

When I returned home, I went to see my doctor. By that time, my blood sugar levels had dropped slightly, but they were still dangerously high at around 300. The doctor was concerned and decided to treat my diabetes aggressively because he wasn't sure how long I had been living with the condition. Along with diabetes medication, he prescribed pills for high blood pressure and kidney function, warning me that I would need to make some serious lifestyle changes.

The diabetes medication I was taking helped to lower my blood sugar, but there was an odd side effect: my body started craving sugar. I found myself eating candy, specifically Skittles, just to keep my blood sugar from dropping too low. I was practically living off candy for a while, which felt strange given that I was supposed to be managing my diabetes. When I went back to my doctor, he reduced my medication, but I was still consuming a lot of sugar to balance out my blood glucose levels. Eventually, he told me to stop taking the diabetes medication entirely because my body no longer needed it.

I was beyond elated! The idea of having to take diabetic pills or insulin injections for the rest of my life had been daunting, and now, I didn't have to. It was a huge relief! Looking back, I was able to connect the dots between the stubborn wound on my thumb and my diabetes diagnosis. Wounds, especially on the extremities, often heal slowly in diabetic patients because high blood sugar levels can impair the body's ability to repair itself. That wound on my finger had been an early sign of a much bigger issue. It wasn't just a simple injury—it was a signal that something deeper was going on in my body.

I found out that once a person is diagnosed with diabetes, there's typically a six-month "honeymoon" period where the condition can seem manageable before it becomes more severe. Many people eventually need insulin to control their blood sugar. But here I am, 10 years later, still managing my diabetes through diet and exercise, without the need for any medication. I realize now that the persistent wound on my thumb was my body's way of telling me that something was wrong, and I'm grateful that I caught it in time to take control of my health.

Hide your sickness, and you will not find healing.

8. Giving Back: A Vision of Service and Gratitude

It all began on August 14, 2008, when my wife and I bought the property on South Wilmington Street. Recently, while passing by the church we rented to the Spanish community, I noticed the building badly needed a fresh coat of paint. As I stood there, staring at its worn-down exterior, I was overwhelmed with gratitude for the many blessings we had received since moving to America. This project felt like the perfect way to give back and show our appreciation to the people of this country.

Our journey began when I was granted a visa to come to the United States, a pivotal moment that transformed my life. Because of that visa, I was able to pursue an education and earn a degree in chemistry. This led to a fulfilling career where I could teach young people the wonders of chemistry—a role I cherished deeply. The opportunities I've had here in America are too numerous to count, but some of the most significant include the birth of my four children. They were all born in the United States, and I'm forever grateful to the nurses, doctors, and hospital staff who brought them into the world safely.

Everything I own, from the house I live in today, to the car I drive, the clothes I wear, the food I eat, and the church I attend, is a direct result of being given a chance here. The warmth and generosity we have received from this country's people are overwhelming! With this gratitude in our hearts, my wife and I began to think about how we could give back. During our time living in Washington, D.C., we had a dear friend who regularly volunteered at a homeless shelter. She invited us to join her, and every Saturday, my job was to wash dishes. It was a simple task, but it ignited a desire in me to do more to serve the homeless. That experience stuck with me, and I began to dream of opening a place where we could serve hot meals to those in need. When we moved to Raleigh, I was determined to find a location that could serve this purpose.

After an extensive search, we found a property on New Bern Avenue that I believed could be the perfect place for a soup kitchen. I wrote a detailed proposal, thoroughly inspected the building, and investigated its potential. Unfortunately, the building wasn't suitable, and despite my best efforts, I had to let go of the idea. But I wasn't discouraged. Soon after, I heard about a property on South Wilmington Street that was up for rent, and I immediately took interest! The rent was higher than the mortgage, but instead of renting, I made an offer to buy the place outright.

There were many hurdles to overcome. I had to secure a loan from a bank and negotiate with the property owner. Thankfully, a real estate agent volunteered his commission and even advocated on my behalf, negotiating to include the parking lot in the deal at no extra cost. It was a huge relief when everything came together, and I was thrilled. We now had a building that could be used not only as a soup kitchen but also as a place of worship for our home church. Another woman, equally passionate about serving the homeless, joined us in this mission.

Once the purchase was finalized, we began renovating the space. It became a family affair. I had just finished the school term in May, so I dedicated all my time to working on the building. My sons and daughter pitched in, and we were fortunate to have a volunteer named Justin who offered his time and energy to help bring our vision to life.

As the renovation progressed, my heart swelled with gratitude. This was not just a building—it was a symbol of the kindness and generosity we had received throughout our lives in the United States. By opening this space, we hoped to give back to the community that had given us so much. When the day finally came to celebrate the building's completion, I stood there, proud of what we had accomplished and excited for the future. The journey had been long and challenging, but it was worth every effort to create a space where people could come together, share a meal, and feel cared for.

Learn to walk before you try to climb a ladder.

9. Building a Soup Kitchen and Serving the Hungry

The renovation process was exhausting, both physically and mentally. The building was in terrible condition when I first received the keys, but we wasted no time getting started. One of the biggest challenges we faced was installing a grease trap, which was essential for the kitchen's operations for a restaurant. Although the building wasn't commercial, serving food meant dealing with grease from washing dishes, and without a proper trap, the plumbing could easily clog.

Originally built as a liquor store and later repurposed as a check-cashing business, the building was overgrown with weeds, cluttered with old furniture, and filled with remnants from its past. The first step was to clear the outside, cutting through the overgrown vegetation. Inside, we hauled away furniture, removed old signs, and completely restructured the space. Luckily, Wake County had several disposal locations for trash and furniture, and I made countless trips in our van, slowly transforming the space.

Once the building was cleaned and gutted, the real work began. Kitchen cabinets was a challenge, but when I called an appliance place, they volunteered to measure and install the cabinets free of charge for the soup kitchen. Plumbing was our top priority; as we connected water to the kitchen, we discovered both bathrooms required extensive renovation. It felt like a never-ending project, especially with the various inspections looming—plumbing, electrical, and the most intimidating of all, the structural inspection. I wanted to build a podium for speakers to stand on during services. I was incredibly nervous, worrying the building might not pass. It felt as though the inspectors were holding us to the same standards as the White House or a governor's mansion, rather than a humble soup kitchen in Raleigh, NC.

The day of the structural inspection finally arrived, and I was bracing myself for bad news. But when the inspector moved the podium and saw that it wasn't attached to the floor, he gave us a passing certificate and an occupancy permit of ninety people, a huge relief, and a major milestone. Fortunately, the carport where we served food didn't require inspection. We were able to quickly pour concrete on the floor, add windows for better lighting, and paint the exterior, transforming it into a functional and welcoming space for our mission.

Once the renovations were complete, the true mission began—feeding the homeless. On the first day, only six people came to eat, but by the next day, that number doubled, and soon we were averaging 70 people a day. The kitchen thrived, offering a comforting and delicious variety of foods—pancakes, grits, oatmeal, scrambled eggs, meatballs, and banana pudding. Guests could enjoy hot coffee, cocoa, or juice. Early arrivals were greeted with honey buns and coffee, creating a warm and welcoming atmosphere. It wasn't just a meal—it was all-you-can-eat, with enough food to take home.

What started as a vision of gratitude blossomed into something much bigger a thriving operation that touched the hearts of the community. Each meal served reflected our core belief: that every person, created in the image of God, deserves dignity, respect, and the security of knowing they won't go hungry. Despite the long hours, obstacles, and physical strain, the joy of seeing lives touched and bellies filled made all the hard work worthwhile.

My role didn't end with the renovations; I was responsible for buying the food needed for breakfast each week and lining up seven volunteers to serve with me in the morning. Every Friday, I'd head to Sam's Club to stock up: 18 dozen eggs, 3 packs of 18 chicken legs, 12 boxes of honey buns, two packs of meatballs, along with milk and wafers for the banana pudding. At home, I would start by roasting the chicken in the oven, preparing the meatballs with barbecue sauce, and baking potatoes. While watching the food in the oven, I'd make the banana pudding. I became known for my cooking, and even now, some of the homeless people I meet tell me how much they miss it. The scrambled eggs, oatmeal, and pancakes were prepared fresh in the morning while the coffee brewed, filling the air with comforting aromas.

Over time, the untouched milk transforms into yogurt.
Prosperity without working heaven without repenting

10. Serving the Homeless

Most of the homeless people I encountered at the soup
kitchen were good-hearted individuals, simply caught in the
tragic circumstances of losing their homes. Life had taken a
tough turn for them, but that didn't change who they were
at their core. Most lived in the woods across the street from
the soup kitchen, finding shelter wherever they could.
Others came from nearby homeless shelters, their lives in
limbo, but still filled with hope.

However, in any group, there are always a few
exceptions. There were one or two individuals who,
because of their mental state or the trauma they carried,
could be dangerous—to themselves or to others. It was for
that reason I decided to put in place a physical barrier—a
window that separated the volunteers from the homeless
guests. This way, volunteers could still serve with
compassion and love, but they were also protected in case
of any unexpected outbursts. Outside, under the carport, the
homeless would sit, enjoying their meals, while the
volunteers worked from inside, serving food through the
window. This arrangement provided a sense of security for
both sides, allowing us to focus on the mission of feeding
those in need without fear.

The diversity of the people who came through our doors
was remarkable. We served people from every continent
and from many different countries. They were
predominantly men, but there were women too, sometimes
accompanied by children. Some of our guests were elderly,
and they carried a certain dignity despite their

circumstances. They came from all walks of life—black, white, Hispanic, Asian—and their stories were as varied as their faces. Each person had their own history, their own struggles, and their own hopes for the future.

Among the regulars were some truly memorable characters. There was one man who always appeared covered in black soot, and his appearance could be intimidating at first. He never said much, but his presence was a constant reminder of the rough conditions many of them lived in. Another man had wild, unruly hair and a long beard that made him look like a king from ancient West Africa. He had a regal air about him, despite his disheveled state. Then, there were those who quickly formed their own small communities, bonding over shared experiences, and finding comfort in each other's company. But just as quickly, others would prefer to keep to themselves, maintaining a quiet distance from the rest, their isolation almost palpable.

One individual who always kept me on high alert was a man who rode his bicycle to the kitchen. He tended to stir up trouble, instigating fights or causing disruptions. Whenever I saw him approach, I would prepare myself for the possibility of conflict. Thankfully, these incidents were rare, but they served as a reminder that homelessness often comes with a host of complex challenges, including mental health issues.

Many of the homeless individuals who came to us were former professionals, people who once had stable lives but had fallen on hard times due to circumstances beyond their control. Some had mental health issues, either due to chemical imbalances or as a result of the rejection and trauma they had experienced throughout their lives. These were people who had once been contributors to society, but a combination of mental health struggles and the harsh economic realities had brought them to the streets.

Raleigh, like many cities, is facing a homelessness crisis. In fact, it takes four minimum-wage workers to afford just one apartment in the area. With the cost of living so high, it's no wonder that nearly 5,000 people in the Raleigh area find themselves without a home. These individuals, despite their circumstances, often carried a quiet resilience, and it was a privilege to serve them. Through it all, I was reminded of the profound importance of kindness, dignity, and respect—things that everyone, regardless of their situation, deserves.

Do good deeds for God, not for rewards from others, and you won't be disappointed.

11. Closing the Hallelujah Soup Kitchen

Serving at the soup kitchen for over 10 years brought me immense personal growth, fulfillment, and a deeper understanding of human connection. From that humble place, in that old building, we served around 150,000 plates of food to the homeless—each plate filled with hot, freshly cooked meals made to taste, completely free of charge. It wasn't just about the food, though. Week after week, we provided a space for people to be fed not only physically but spiritually as well. Over the years, I preached more than 400 sermons to the homeless, standing at the same location in the carport. It became a place where I could share words of hope and encouragement, meeting people right where they were in life.

While they waited for breakfast to be ready, we served hot coffee and honey buns, which became a little tradition. The consistency of showing up every week earned me a place in their hearts. We served with care and quality, and I often heard people say that our coffee was better than Starbucks and our breakfasts rivaled the Pancake House. This simple affirmation meant the world to me because it wasn't just about feeding people; it was about giving them dignity. We wanted them to know they were valued, and it showed in the meals we prepared.

Transportation was also part of the service we provided. Using my van, I would transport people from the nearby shelter to the soup kitchen and back. We jokingly called it the "Jesus Taxi." It became more than a vehicle for transport—it symbolized a lifeline for those who had nowhere else to turn, ensuring they wouldn't miss out on a warm meal and the sense of community we fostered.

Another significant benefit I gained was the chance to connect people—especially volunteers—with an opportunity to serve those they might typically avoid. Many volunteers were Christians who longed to fulfill the biblical commandment: "I was hungry, and you fed me; I was thirsty, and you gave me drink." This command resonates deeply, but for various reasons, including safety concerns and discomfort, many people stay away from directly engaging with the homeless. Through the soup kitchen, we created a safe, structured environment where volunteers could offer their help while feeling secure. In 2019, we made the difficult decision to turn in our license and 501(c)(3) status, just before the pandemic hit. It was an incredibly heart-wrenching choice, especially since the soup kitchen had become so deeply intertwined with my life's purpose and spiritual service. For over a decade, the kitchen wasn't just a place to feed the hungry—it was a beacon of hope, community, and a reflection of my personal mission to serve others. Closing it felt like closing a chapter of my life that had shaped me in profound ways.

Informing the volunteers was one of the hardest parts of the process. Many of them had been with us for years, showing up every week with the same commitment and passion I had. For some, it was their first consistent experience working with the homeless, and for others, it had become a personal ministry. Breaking the news that we were closing was incredibly emotional. Even to this day, people approach me and ask when they can come back to volunteer, holding on to the memories and bonds they had formed through the years. The sense of community we built wasn't easily forgotten, and neither was the need.

After deciding to close the soup kitchen, preparing the building for rent was an exhausting and emotional task. Years of service had left a mark on the space, and clearing out the storage rooms and supplies brought back memories of the countless meals served and the lives touched. With the help of a dedicated team, the building was thoroughly cleaned and repainted, ready for a new chapter. The church that rented the space continued the mission of serving the homeless, offering meals to those in need, which brought comfort knowing the work I started was still making an impact.

Though I stepped away from leading the soup kitchen, the heart of the mission endured. The building remains a place of refuge, and the values of love and service continue to thrive. The experience left a lasting impression on me, showing that even when we step back, the good we do has the power to ripple out and touch lives in unexpected ways. Serving the homeless became a mission that united us all in kindness and faith, reminding us that we are all God's children, no matter our circumstances.

12. Attack on My Kidneys and My Heart

Two years ago, during a routine checkup, my doctor found microscopic blood in my urine. At the time, he didn't think it was a cause for concern. However, during my next checkup, where they performed another blood test and urine analysis, the results were the same—microscopic blood in the urine. My primary physician suggested we wait for another test before taking any action. Three months later, the results came back, once again showing blood in my urine. This time, my doctor referred me to a urologist for further evaluation.

The urologist conducted another urine test and confirmed the bleeding. He then prescribed a CAT scan to check my kidneys for stones and did a procedure to examine my bladder and prostate. Fortunately, the results were positive—the bladder was healthy, and though the prostate was slightly enlarged, it wasn't a cause for concern. The scan revealed a small 2 mm kidney stone, but the urologist decided it wasn't large enough to require any surgical intervention.

Not wanting to take any risks, I went to an herbal medicine store and asked for a remedy for kidney stones. They recommended Chanca Piedra, an herbal supplement known for breaking down stones. I started taking it faithfully, mixing it with my water three times a day. When I went back to my doctor for a follow-up, the bleeding had completely stopped, and there was no more blood in my urine. I was so happy and felt sure the Chanca Piedra had worked. The urologist, who often must give bad news, was pleased with my results and told me to celebrate by treating myself to some ice cream.

Around the same time, I experienced another health scare while visiting Tenu's relatives in Texas. One morning, I felt dizzy and was taken to urgent care, where they immediately performed an EKG. Without hesitation, they referred me to the emergency room at a nearby hospital. After a series of tests, the doctors couldn't find anything wrong but recommended I follow up with a cardiologist when I got back home.

Upon returning, I consulted my primary physician, who referred me to a cardiologist. The cardiologist ordered a nuclear stress test, which provides imaging to see how blood flows to the heart during rest and exercise. Thankfully, the results were negative. The cardiologist gave me two great news: my heart was strong, pumping blood effectively, and there was no blockage in my arteries. Hearing this brought me immense relief. I was overjoyed to learn that both my kidneys and heart were in good health. The stress I had been carrying for weeks suddenly lifted, and I was filled with gratitude for the good news.

Patience will help us avoid many problems.

13. The Bittersweet Reality of Letting Go: A Daughter's Move to the West Coast

When our daughter moved to West Coast for her new job working with refugees, it triggered a wave of emotions for Tenu and me. The first week passed almost unnoticed, as we were busy traveling to Virginia Beach for a family reunion and attending several church events. But as the days went on, the reality of her absence began to sink in. For Tenu, it started yesterday at church, where she was suddenly overwhelmed by a barrage of feelings, leading to uncontrollable tears. I sat next to her, trying my best to comfort her, but this morning was different. We both woke up feeling sad, the weight of our daughter's move finally hitting us.

We've experienced empty nest syndrome before, especially when our children left one by one for college. Our second daughter moved to Greensboro, and my brother-in-law bought a house and moved out. It's been eight years since my mother-in-law, who was an integral part of our family and a second mother to our children, passed away. Over the years, we've watched our children grow up, marry, and start their own families. When our oldest son moved to the greater Washington area, we didn't fully consider the distance we would have to bear in our old age to see him and his wife. While we're incredibly proud of them, the physical distance between us has been a constant reminder of the changes in our lives. Our grandchildren in Raleigh are busy with school and after-school activities, and the other two lovely and precious grandsons who live an hour away. Visiting our grandchildren in Arizona requires a plane trip, adding yet another layer of separation.

Now, with our daughter moving to West coast, the realization that she is no longer close by has deepened our sense of loss. Every time Tenu gets excited, our daughter would say "teregagi," an Amharic word meaning "calm down." She also inherited a dog from her friend named Lola, who is so cute and friendly. The fellowship we once enjoyed feels diminished, and we are left adjusting to life without her daily presence. There's a deep sadness as we come to terms with this new reality, but also a sense of pride. Our daughter has grown into a strong, independent woman who now owns her own home and has taken on significant responsibilities. Yet, this pride is mingled with anxiety. She's venturing into uncharted territory, and as parents, we can't help but worry about her safety, health, and happiness.

She's always been someone who easily forms and builds relationships, but knowing that she's in a new place, likely feeling lonely in the first few months, adds to our concern. The past few years, she's been heavily involved in our lives, and not having her around now feels like an unexpected loss. This mix of sadness, pride, worry, and excitement creates a complex emotional experience that we're still learning to navigate. We miss hearing "teregagi," we miss Lola, and most of all, we miss our daughter. This morning, Tenu and I cried a little, held hands, hugged each other, and exchanged words of comfort.

The seed blooms according to the soil it's planted in.

14. Exceeding Expectations: 40th Anniversary Reflection

November 11 is a date forever etched in my heart—my wedding anniversary. As this special day approaches, a wave of reflections, questions, and anticipations stir within me. I think back to a time when I was single, living in Washington, D.C., working at Georgetown University, with my education behind me and my future ahead, filled with the endless possibilities of youth.

My mother, with the wisdom only a mother possesses, visited me during this time. She immediately sensed that something was missing in my life. She knew I needed a partner, someone to share my journey with, and in her quiet determination, she set out to find me a wife. She reached out to mothers she had met on the airplane, at the Orthodox Church, and through various connections. Suddenly, I found myself being introduced to a parade of prospective young ladies; none of whom seemed to match what I was looking for.

Finally, perhaps out of frustration with my reluctance, my mother asked me directly, "What are your expectations?" We were sitting on a bench in a quiet section of a shopping mall, and I responded with a list of five qualities that mattered most to me. I told her that my future wife needed to be light skinned like her, speak my mother's language, love me more than any other man, be a Christian, and, share my culture. These were my expectations, carefully thought out and deeply rooted in my upbringing and beliefs.

When my mother returned to Ethiopia, she didn't forget her commitment to find me a wife. A few weeks later, she sent me two photographs of a woman she believed fit my description. I examined the pictures, but like buying clothes or shoes online, I couldn't decide based solely on a picture. Living in America, a land of freedom and choice, I found the idea of an arranged marriage impossible to accept. I anticipated a life where love was discovered, not arranged, and where mutual choice and affection guided such a profound decision.

Yet, despite my hesitation, the wheels were in motion on the other side of the world. My family in Ethiopia progressed with the arrangements, and before long, they had agreed to introduce her to the entire family. I remained skeptical, unsure if this was the right path for me. The anticipation of what was to come filled me with both excitement and doubt. Could this really be the woman I would spend my life with? Was she truly the one who would fulfill my expectations?

To answer these questions, we decided to meet in Nairobi, away from the political turmoil in Ethiopia. Tenu, the woman my mother had chosen, had already met everyone in the family and had been warmly accepted. I took a two-week vacation from work, left my sister in Washington, D.C., and traveled to Kenya. The anticipation of meeting her in person was intense. We finally met at a family's home in Nairobi, and Tenu joined me at the Milimani Hotel, where I had booked a one-bedroom apartment.

Upon meeting her, I was struck by her beauty. Yet,
doubts crept in. I was 14 years her senior, and I couldn't
shake the feeling that our marriage might not work because
of the age difference. As the days passed, I found myself
questioning everything. But one morning, as I sat in a
Catholic Church in downtown Nairobi, I reflected deeply on
the question my mother had once asked me: "What are your
expectations?" The next day, all my fears and doubts
disappeared, and it was in that quiet moment of reflection
that I realized Tenu met every one of my qualifications and
exceeded my expectations. She was everything I had asked
for and more. After exchanging vows, we began building a
romantic relationship that deepened each day into a
profound and natural love. I returned to the United States,
filled with a sense of hope and anticipation for the life we
would build together when she will get a visa and come and
join me in Washington, D.C.

Now, forty years have passed. We've raised four
children, who are now married with families of their own,
and we have the joy of several grandchildren. As I look
back on our life together, I find myself pondering a question
I had never considered before: Do I meet her expectations?
As our anniversary approaches, this question, simple yet
profound, lingers in my heart. It's a reminder that love is
not only about finding someone who meets your ideals but
also about striving to be the partner they deserve.

After all these years, my devotion to being the husband
Tenu deserves remains unwavering. As our 40th
anniversary draws near, I am overwhelmed with gratitude
for the incredible journey we have shared and the life we

have built together. I hope Tenu sees that my greatest priority in life is to continually meet and exceed her expectations as a husband, honoring the love and commitment that have defined our years together.

A supportive wife, a joyful life..

15. <u>The Canine Chronicles and From Poison Ivy to Personal Growth</u>

My morning walks have led me to meet a variety of dogs and their owners, each with its unique story and personality. Considering there are around 900 million dogs worldwide, it's interesting to think that only a small fraction of them forms meaningful connections with humans. However, the ones I've encountered have each taught me something valuable.

One of the most memorable dogs I've met is Coco, a resilient three-legged dog. I first met her a while back, and I saw her again this morning. Despite her obvious exhaustion, Coco still eagerly wanted to walk in the park. Her owner shared with me the heartbreaking story of how a truck ran over Coco's leg, leaving her stranded. The injury was so severe that the doctors had to amputate, yet Coco has adapted to life with three legs. Initially, the owner tried getting her a support wheel, but Coco didn't like it. Instead, she learned to walk and even enjoyed covering at least a mile each day. Coco has learned to do more with less and her desire to survive despite her limitations inspired me to push through my challenges, knowing that perseverance can lead to remarkable outcomes.

Another dog I've come to know is Gracie, a spirited hunting dog from the American Foxhound class. Gracie has a strong instinct for chasing squirrels, which seems to be her primary focus during our encounters. Whenever she spots me, she runs over, eager for her daily rub. While Gracie is always enthusiastic, her true passion lies in the hunt. Her single-minded determination to chase squirrels reminds me of the joy that comes from following our destiny, no matter how small or insignificant they may seem to others.

Lastly, there's Lucky, a massive, wrinkled-faced Chinese dog who is both imposing and friendly. Lucky's size is enough to make anyone cautious, and I often worry he might accidentally jump on me and cause injury. His owner is always careful to shorten the leash as we approach, ensuring that I'm safe. Despite his size, Lucky has a gentle side—he loves to have his back rubbed and always presents it to me when we meet. Lucky has figured the balance between strength and gentleness. While his size offers protection, it's his calm and obedience fosters trust and attachment. Lucky knows when to be gentle and caring and also fierce for protection.

Each of these dogs—Coco, Gracie, and Lucky—has left an imprint on me. Coco's resilience, Gracie's passion, and Lucky's balance between strength and gentleness are lessons that extend far beyond our daily interactions. These encounters have deepened my appreciation for the unique qualities that each dog brings into the world, and the ways in which they reflect important truths about life.

When your blessing is as expansive as the heavens, your quests will be as countless as the stars

16. <u>From Poison Ivy to Personal Growth:
Confronting the Past to Cultivate Creativity</u>

When I got home this morning, I went outside to tackle the poison ivy that had grown so tall it was now reaching the window. From my kitchen, I could see it climbing up the wall, seemingly growing taller by the day. Initially, I thought a shovel would be enough, but I quickly realized the weed eater would be more effective. I also grabbed an axe to dig into the ground.

In that same flower garden, I encountered some aggressive plants not only poison ivy, but rose bushes, monkey grass, and alpha grass with spreading runners. Poison ivy, in particular, is notorious for the problems it causes. I learned that even indirect exposure—such as burning the plant and inhaling the smoke from a mile away—can lead to severe itching, swelling, and, in extreme cases, difficulty breathing. The plant produces special oil that triggers allergic reactions in about 85% of people.

At the beginning I couldn't reach the entire bed of poison ivy, I did manage to get to the roses. I carefully pruned them, mindful of the thorns, and only trimmed away the dried parts. While using the weed eater, I had to be particularly cautious of the grounding wire that runs around the house, which protects against lightning strikes. It kept getting in the way, so I had to hold it up. As I dug up most of the poison ivy roots and detached the vines from the wall, I learned just how tenacious this plant can be. Poison ivy has a way of clinging to surfaces with its hairy roots, making it difficult to remove. I also dug up regular grass and monkey grass, both of which are aggressive plants that can quickly overtake a garden. Clearing the ground about a foot away from the building, I made my way around the yard, reflecting on the importance of maintaining clear boundaries to prevent unwanted growth.

When I finished, I had gathered a pile of rose clippings, monkey grass, and regular grass. I plan to clean up the pile in the afternoon when I can catch my breath, and the sun goes down. Through this process, I found what I was looking for, a lesson or two in the importance of using the right tools for the job, the need for caution and awareness of potential hazards, the value of persistence in overcoming challenges, and the significance of proper timing and planning.

King Solomon said there's a time for everything, and that includes taking care of my yard. I enjoy mowing the grass because it not only keeps my yard looking nice, but it also gives me 2-3 hours of good exercise. In the summer, I mow once every two weeks at the start of the season, then switch to once a week as the grass grows faster. When it rains, the grass grows even quicker, but if I don't clean up the clippings, they pile up and smother the healthy grass underneath. This taught me a lesson: just like the clippings can harm the grass, ignoring past mistakes can block my creativity. It's like the poison ivy in my yard—if I don't pull it out by the roots, it will take over. In the same way, I need to deal with my past mistakes. It's hard work, requiring honesty and courage, but if I don't do it, my creativity will be held back.

Wisdom is more valuable than physical strength.

17. Family Reunion

This year's family reunion at Virginia Beach was a continuation of a tradition that has been going strong for 12 years. Family reunions like ours are not just about gathering for a meal—they represent a commitment to maintaining and strengthening family bonds. Gathering people for a family reunion can be challenging due to busy schedules, driving distance, financial constraints, family conflicts, and health issues, particularly for older family members. Our family reunion stays together through the leadership of strong family members who organize gatherings, resolve conflicts, and ensure everyone feels included. Their efforts in maintaining communication, tradition, and a focus on family unity help preserve the bond despite busy schedules and distance. Our family gatherings, held twice a year at spring and summer, are deeply rooted in the importance of togetherness. These reunions offer more than just a day of fun; they are an opportunity to reconnect, preserve our culture, and pass down traditions to the younger generation. The tradition of assigning food duties, with each family contributing their favorite dishes, adds to the sense of community and shared responsibility. This year, as always, we had a mix of good food, from injera to lasagna, reflecting our diverse tastes and backgrounds.

Each family arranges their own hotel reservations, but we all meet at the beach around lunchtime. One generous family member always brings the tent, and though setting up the tent and chairs takes some time, it's worth it for the comfort it provides throughout the day. From swimming in the ocean to singing gospel songs, every activity is a reminder of the bonds we share. Each gathering is a celebration of our shared history and a step toward preserving our legacy for future generations.

I'm usually asked to start with a prayer, followed by another person, and then we often have gospel singing from the Orthodox Church. The beach activities are a highlight—many of us enjoy getting our feet wet or swimming in the ocean, while others sit, talk, and take pictures. There's a $100 membership fee per family, which the secretary collects to cover the expenses for dinner. The younger family members are tasked with finding a restaurant that can accommodate our large group, which can be a challenge with over 20 people, but we always manage. The children are still young enough to attend family gatherings, but as they get older, they are less likely to come despite our best efforts to encourage them. We've tried everything to keep them involved, but their interests and commitments are pulling them away.

Once we find a spot, we gather in the evening for dinner. The meal is more than just food—it's a time for fellowship, fun, and deepening our family bonds before we depart for the night. These reunions have taught me the importance of family, commitment, and the joy of coming together, no matter the challenges. Each gathering strengthens our connections and creates memories that we cherish year after year.

A house without people is like a barn without animals.

18. <u>Decision to Re-strategize</u>

This morning, I was really challenged by the idea of having a strategy for my work with Hallelujah Adult Daycare Center. For many years, people my age have often believed that simply asking for blessings and waiting would bring the results we want. But I've come to understand that just waiting isn't enough. I have the ability to think, plan, and take action, and it's time for me to start using that.

A Nigerian preacher's advice struck a chord with me: he concluded that the prosperity gospel has failed in Nigeria and instead of putting undue pressure on self, the preacher suggested to re-strategize. Reflecting on my vision for Hallelujah Adult Daycare, I remembered the advice my brother gave me—to create a detailed business plan. I did so with enthusiasm, but reality hit hard when I discovered that maintaining the daycare would cost over $100,000 per year, far beyond my means and expertise, especially when the users wouldn't be paying.

This led me to consider Zacchaeus's story, who, despite his limitations, found a way to see Jesus by climbing a sycamore tree. His determination to overcome obstacles and position himself for success inspired me. I realized that I, too, need to re-strategize, seek out resources, and position myself to succeed, rather than waiting passively. Just as Zacchaeus took bold steps, I must act decisively, leveraging the opportunities before me. I'm learning to stay open to unexpected outcomes and be prepared for life-changing moments that come from stepping out in faith.

The journey with Hallelujah Adult Daycare is restarting again this morning. What I've learned is that I must re-strategize to overcome the needed funds and find resources for finding qualified help. I'm committed to applying these lessons: strategizing, trusting in God's power, and taking calculated risks. I envision God's power and my efforts as essential, like the electricity needed to light a lamp, the fuel required for a car to move, or the battery necessary for a smartphone to function. Therefore, I am up again to re-strategize to revamp my plans for the adult day care.

When you hit your noise your eyes cry.

19. <u>A Funeral Service</u>

A former church member's funeral was a deeply moving experience. When one of his daughters asked me to pray and speak at both the church and the cemetery, I was given just two days' notice. Preparing for such an important occasion took everything within me, but I was honored to be a part of it. My task was to reflect on what my 90-year-old friend might have said about each of his children. The responsibility felt heavy, yet it was a privilege to contribute to his final farewell, to express the love and pride he undoubtedly had for his family.

Speaking at the funeral was an emotional challenge. I cared deeply about the deceased, and the weight of honoring his memory while comforting his grieving family was almost overwhelming. Fear and doubt in my ability to do justice to the occasion began to paralyze me. Yet, I knew this was also an opportunity to offer personal reflections and stories that would bring comfort to those mourning his loss. By sharing memories and celebrating a life well-lived, I hoped to help his loved ones find solace. As I prepared, I reminded myself that I was speaking to people who knew and loved him, just as I did, and that gave me a sense of peace.

To ease some of my nerves, I attended the wake on Thursday. It was held just down the street from where I lived, and it was an opportunity to meet his children, some of whom had traveled from overseas, as well as other family members. The experience was eye-opening, reminding me that my words were not just for strangers but for people who shared a deep connection with this man. It gave me a renewed sense of purpose and made me feel more comfortable about the task ahead.

On Friday, during the funeral service, I found myself multitasking. Our university president had scheduled a meeting to announce the approval of a crucial loan, and I was torn between focusing on that good news and preparing my speech for the service. In the end, I decided to share the news with the congregation, as many were aware of the financial stress at the university and welcomed the relief. When it was my turn to speak, I began by posing a question: "What would the deceased say about his children?" It was a heartfelt moment as I honored each of his children, beginning with the eldest son and his wife, who had taken on the responsibility of caring for their elderly parents' property and representing the family.

At the cemetery, I led the family in a collective expression of love and gratitude. Many of those 13 children and 23 grandchildren may have wanted to say something in the service I gave them chance to express their feelings to their father. I asked them to repeat after me and say, "We love you, daddy, we miss you already, thank you for giving us life, and thank you for sharing quality time with us." It was a powerful, emotional moment of closure. After the service, the children didn't want to leave the cemetery and lingering at the funeral sight singing and, I went to the gym to unwind and reflect on the day. It was a day filled with both sorrow and beauty, a day to honor the life of a man who had been a significant part of our previous church community. *You can't use help if it is not there when you need it.*

20.   50th <u>Year Celebration!</u>

Today, I had the honor of attending my friends' 50th
wedding anniversary, often called a Golden Anniversary.
Another person and I were asked to serve as ushers at the
celebration, a small but meaningful contribution to this
special day. This milestone marked half a century of shared
experiences, memories, and growth—not just as individuals
but as partners on a lifelong journey. It was more than a
celebration of their enduring love; it was a recognition of
the resilience, dedication, and mutual respect that have
allowed their relationship to thrive over the years.

The husband wanted a simple cookies and coffee
ceremony, but his wife wanted a full-blown celebration,
with Kingsley highchairs for the two, sit down-eating with
full course dinner, and complete church service. The
husband gave in and overlooked his desire because reaching
the 50-year mark in a marriage is truly remarkable. It
speaks to their commitment to one another, their ability to
compromise, and their shared values.

The celebration featured a beautiful slideshow that took
us through five decades of their lives together. From raising
children to supporting each other through careers, illnesses,
and other life challenges, they've shared countless moments
that have only strengthened their bond. Each year together
has deepened their relationship, enriching their
understanding and appreciation of one another.

One story that stood out was shared by the husband. He
recounted how he had been serving in the church without
initially noticing his future wife, to say it in a very

diplomatic way. It wasn't until one day, when his eyes suddenly opened, that he saw her in a new light. He quickly arranged a meeting and asked for her hand in marriage. She requested time to think and pray about it. The next day, from a distance, she gave him her answer—a quiet yet confident "I agree with your request." Looking back at their wedding photos, it was touching to see how much he had changed over the years, while she seemed to have remained remarkably the same.

Attending the 50th wedding anniversary celebration offered me valuable insights into what sustains a strong and enduring relationship. Faith played a crucial role in the couple's marriage, as their shared spiritual foundation helped them stay united through adversity. This highlighted the importance of a mutual moral or spiritual anchor in a relationship. Additionally, the celebration emphasized the power of community. The couple's deep connections with their church and extended family reminded me how vital it is to nurture relationships beyond marriage, as a strong support network can provide encouragement and strength during tough times.

The event showed just how important gratitude and humility are. The couple's sincere thanks to everyone who supported them over the years reminded me how valuable it is to acknowledge the love and help of those around us. As they reflected on their 50 years together, I couldn't help but think about my own upcoming 40th wedding anniversary. Their enduring love inspired me to appreciate how relationships grow and deepen over time, whether through adventures, returning to Ethiopia, or simply enjoying quiet moments together. It proves that one man can stay committed to one woman for a lifetime. This is a moment to honor the past, cherish the present, and look forward with hope. Their love story will continue to inspire and uplift others for years to come.

What you put in is what you get out.

21. <u>From Molars to Implants: Navigating Life's Changes with Research and Resilience</u>

I have enjoyed having beautiful teeth all my life. However, as I aged, I began to lose my molar teeth. The first time I had a molar pulled, it felt like I had lost a part of myself, something that could never be regained. Even though I didn't use these molar teeth, the sense of loss was significant. Over the years, more of my back teeth disappeared, one by one. I gradually adjusted to this loss, adapting because my diet didn't require heavy chewing.

The situation became more challenging when I broke one of my front teeth, though the dentist was able to restore it. But when a second front tooth broke off at the gum line, it was clear that I needed to consider dentures or implants. The first estimate I received for implants was $40,000, and the second was even higher at $60,000. These costs were staggering, and I soon realized I need to do thorough research for such a significant decision. Through diligent investigation, I found that the same quality of implants could be obtained overseas for as low as $23,000. I must also include transportation costs, food and hotels. Exploring international options, I was able to find an affordable and high-quality service; but it has its downfall. There are significant drawbacks to consider, including varying quality of care, potential communication barriers, and inadequate follow-up care, and insurance limitations. Currently I am contemplating between getting a dental implant or settling for dentures.

Your lips and teeth work together to create a beautiful smile.

22. Skin Burn

When I was working as a teacher at SAU, I had a habit
of drinking tea throughout the day. In the mornings, I
preferred caffeinated Lipton tea because it helped wake me
up and gave me the energy to get through the busy hours. In
the afternoons, I switched to something more calming—
Bengal Spice tea by the Celestial Seasonings company,
which is decaffeinated and packed with cinnamon and other
aromatic spices. I loved how the warmth of the tea and the
rich spices gave me a boost without the need for more
caffeine.

In my office, I would use an electric kettle to boil water
for the tea. However, I noticed that the tea wasn't steeping
well. The color was too light, and the spices didn't seem to
extract fully from the Bengal Spice tea. I tried an
experiment: after boiling the water, I would put the cup of
tea into the microwave and boil it again. That extra heat did
the trick! The tea's color became richer, and the spices were
fully extracted, filling my office with the lovely, warm
smell of cinnamon and other spices. Anytime someone
walked into my office, they would comment on how good it
smelled, like a cozy kitchen on a winter day.

One afternoon, while preparing my usual tea, I used a
Styrofoam cup, which I normally don't use. I boiled the
water in my electric kettle, poured it over the tea bag, and
then placed the cup in the microwave to get it extra hot.
After the microwave finished, I reached in to take out the
cup, but I hadn't noticed that some of the cream I added had
spilled out, making the cup slippery. As I picked it up, the

hot teacup slipped out of my hands and landed right on my lap. The tea wasn't just hot—it had been boiled twice, and it was scalding.

In a moment of panic, I quickly jumped up and tried to clean off the boiling tea from my leg. The pain was immediate and intense, and I could feel my skin burning. Even though I cleaned it up as best I could, the damage was done. My skin was already blistering from the heat. I called my brother for advice, and he recommended using a burn cream to help heal the skin. I diligently applied the cream for at least a week, but despite my efforts, the burn left a darkened scar on my leg. I even tried covering it up with more cream to lighten the scar, but nothing seemed to work.

The whole experience was painful and frustrating, not just because of the injury but because it left a permanent mark on my skin. Every time I saw the scar, it reminded me to be more careful, especially when handling anything hot. It was a hard lesson learned from something as simple as making a cup of tea.

Many axes lie in wait for a fallen tree.

23. <u>Prayer is Central to Receiving Healing!</u>

When it comes to health, I've accepted that our world isn't perfect, and my body has its flaws. When I asked my 86-year-old uncle about health, he said, "Pain is everywhere." His words made me think about what I might face at his age. However, over the years, I've seen the amazing results of my prayers and those of others, showing me that God's healing power is real. The Gospel teaches me to pray in every situation—whether I'm happy or suffering—but I struggle to keep my faith strong.

Living a long life brings many health challenges. It's easier to let go of money and status but giving up health is much harder. When my muscles hurt, I try to see it as a chance to ask God for help, whether that healing comes quickly or takes time. For me, healing comes in different ways: taking my medicine, resting, or through divine intervention. I believe God's healing power didn't end in the past; it is still here today. However, it can be hard to deal with the fact that not every prayer for healing is answered the way I want, which tests my faith.

I've witnessed many healings in my life. Once, I prayed for a woman in a coma at Duke Hospital, and after joining with a friend, she came out of the coma. Later, she earned her master's degree in theology. I also prayed for a man possessed by a demon while we were at a dollar store, and he was set free. I've prayed for women trying to get pregnant, and many of them succeeded. One woman even showed me her new Lexus, reminding me that I had prayed for her in the past. People looking for jobs returned after a few days to tell me they found work. At one time, asking for miracles felt as easy as putting a drivable car in reverse—it will just go backward. I find comfort in hearing about other healings, but recently, miraculous healings seem less common.

I also find comfort when our whole congregation prays together; the care we show each other is soothing, even if we don't see immediate healing. This makes me wonder if we're doing something wrong or if our faith has weakened. Whether through group prayers or families dealing with illness, combining faith, prayer, and practical actions is important for healing.

Medicine is a gift from God, much like fuel for our life's journey, but prayer connects us to the true source of healing. I enjoy being part of healing services at church and feeling the Holy Spirit's presence, but I also recognize the importance of both spiritual and natural remedies. Still, I constantly struggle with the tension between faith and doubt, hoping that in time, God will reveal His perfect plan for healing.

A person with strong ambition and faith in their dreams will find a way to overcome their challenges.

24. <u>The Importance of Leaving a Place Better Than We Found It</u>

This morning, I am overwhelmed with the cleaning and painting that my neighbor left for me to handle. As someone who knows all too well the demands of moving, I anticipated the challenges they would face, but I never expected this. Moving is one of life's most taxing experiences, requiring not just physical effort but also a deep sense of responsibility. Over the years, I've experienced my fair share of relocations—fourteen moves in total. My journey has taken me to various places: I lived in Washington, DC, for six months, then in Baltimore for two and a half years, and returned to Washington, DC, where I stayed for 16 years. Since 1990, I've made my home in Raleigh, NC. In each of these locations, I moved two or three times. Despite these frequent changes, one thing has always remained constant—I've made it a priority to leave each place as I found it, if not better. I made it a purpose to clean, organize, and ensure everything was in order before saying my final goodbyes, following the simple wisdom that "a clean house is a sign of a clean mind."

Last Saturday, some friends of ours moved out of the apartment, and I was prepared to help them with the usual post-move cleanup. However, what I encountered was far beyond what I expected. Their once orderly home was now in chaos, with boxes scattered everywhere, clothes in disarray, and their son's toys packed away in numerous containers. Moving is undoubtedly overwhelming, and I understand the struggle of dealing with boxes, furniture, and personal belongings. However, what I couldn't comprehend was the mess they left behind.

I had given them a brand-new stove and nearly new refrigerator, along with a new sink and kitchen cabinet. But when I walked into the apartment the morning after they moved, I was shocked by what I saw. The floor was dirty, the walls were in poor condition, and the bathroom and kitchen were in a disgraceful state. I couldn't help but ask myself—what went wrong?

I know these friends well. The wife knows how to clean; we had even helped her secure a cleaning job in the past, where she had excelled. The husband works in construction, a field where attention to detail and cleanup is crucial. So how did things deteriorate so badly? What happened to the sense of responsibility, care, and consciousness that should have guided them? What happened to their respect for the space they were leaving behind?

In America, and really anywhere, there's an unspoken rule about moving out: we should leave a place clean. We shouldn't leave without cleaning up, especially the kitchen and bathroom. It's not just about being tidy; it's about showing respect—for us, for others, and for the homes we've lived in. That's why I felt so disappointed—not only in how they left the apartment but also in the broken trust and lack of respect for the values we've always shared. Someone told me that in six months, the new house they bought will be just as messy because that's how they live. Moving can be tough but leaving a place in good condition is the least we can do to show respect for what we've been given and for those who will live there after us.

25. Transforming a Deceitful Heart: A Journey Toward Spiritual Renewal

I've been struggling with the meaning of the scripture, "The heart is deceitful above all things and desperately wicked" (Jeremiah 17:9). It makes me question if my own heart is truly deceitful and, if so, how I can change it and live with that knowledge. This reflection affects how I understand human nature and my own behavior, especially in terms of personal growth and spiritual transformation. I'm also grappling with how to discern truth from falsehood within myself. Despite these challenges, I believe that transformation is possible through God's grace, and faith plays a key role in overcoming the deceitfulness described in the scripture.

The first step to improving myself is accepting that, like everyone else, my heart can sometimes lead me in the wrong direction. I may think I'm doing the right thing, but deep down, I can be driven by selfishness or make choices that end up being harmful. Acknowledging this helps me start changing for the better. After that, I need to reflect honestly and ask for help in understanding where I've gone wrong. It takes humility to admit my weaknesses, but it's necessary for growth.

I also need to recognize that I can't fix everything on my own. Real transformation comes when I let go of control and open myself up to change. This isn't a one-time event—it's something I have to work on every day. By doing this, I allow new, healthier habits and perspectives to form, which guide my actions and decisions.

Once I've started this process, it's important to stay focused and let my positive choices guide me. Instead of relying on old ways of thinking, I make a conscious effort to listen to the inner voice that steers me toward what's right. This means staying aware, reflecting, and being open to learning each day.

In the end, change takes time, but with persistence and self-awareness, I can move away from harmful habits and live with more clarity and purpose. It's a journey, but each step forward brings me closer to being the person I strive to be, making choices that align with my values instead of my old, flawed ways. Every day is a chance to make better decisions and grow into a more fulfilled, peaceful version of myself.

26. Working with People at the Soup Kitchen

The first lesson learned at the soup kitchen was the importance of teamwork and the various roles people play in making a mission successful. There were four main groups involved: the volunteers who showed up early to serve breakfast, the donors who provided financial support, the church members who ensured the mission aligned with the church's values, and the homeless people who were served. Each group contributed in their own way to the overall operation, creating a diverse and collaborative environment focused on service and compassion.

Working at the soup kitchen followed a system that divided responsibilities efficiently. The person at the window played a key role by interacting with each guest and helping keep the line moving. Volunteers also handled specific tasks like serving coffee, oatmeal, and hot meals. There was flexibility among the volunteers, with everyone ready to step in where needed. The floater role involved guiding volunteers, interacting with the homeless, and helping newcomers feel comfortable, creating a sense of teamwork and connection.

One of the most rewarding aspects was seeing volunteers, particularly young people, come together to serve. Teenagers, families, and even churches from nearby areas brought their children to volunteer, instilling values of empathy and generosity. Some volunteers had deeply personal reasons for serving, such as honoring lost loved ones. The soup kitchen became a place of healing for many, and it was touching to witness families and individuals come together in acts of kindness.

While the contributions of volunteers were greatly valued, the decision was made not to allow homeless people to serve, as they were meant to receive care during their time of need. However, dedicated support from groups like the local Korean church, which provided clothing and food during the holiday season, and a choir from MIT, who traveled to spread positivity through hymns and service, showcased the broader community's commitment to supporting the mission. These efforts brought joy and unity to the soup kitchen during critical times.
Ultimately, the soup kitchen experience became a meaningful journey of service and connection. Meeting people from all walks of life and working alongside volunteers who brought their unique stories was a powerful reminder of shared humanity. In serving others, the soup kitchen not only provided meals but also created a community where kindness and compassion thrived, leaving a lasting impact on everyone involved.

A greedy heart cannot know love.

27. I Miss Teaching!

Last night, I was speaking with a high school student, and as she prepared to begin her journey in high school, I told her that I had just finished my teaching career. Even though the university where I taught had its share of problems, I deeply miss teaching. I miss the rich interactions with students, the engaging discussions with colleagues, and the process of preparing my lectures. Standing in front of the class, delivering material, and seeing the light of understanding in my students' eyes brought me great fulfillment.

One of the greatest joys of teaching was being around young people. Their fresh ideas and creative minds were a source of inspiration for an old man like me. They pushed me to think in new ways and to stay energetic and curious. In my classes, we followed strict rules, like no cell phone use or wearing hats. I usually had over 50 students in each class, many of them first-year students or early college attendees. I assign a lot of homework, which had to be turned in at the beginning of each class, with no late work accepted. I gave them a detailed schedule at the start of the semester, so there were no surprises. Despite this, students often came up with countless excuses for not turning in their assignments on time, something that never ceased to amaze me.

I held five exams throughout the semester, with a comprehensive final exam at the end. The final was set by the school, and many students tried to buy their tickets home for Christmas break early, hoping to avoid the exam.

But by the end of the semester, they were accustomed to the routine of homework, exams, and the importance of class attendance. The first two weeks of class were always dedicated to learning their names, getting to know who they are, and understanding their goals in life. I also created an attendance sheet for every class, which has been a lifesaver. At the bottom of this sheet, I would list all the assignment due dates and exam dates, ensuring there was no confusion. Students signed it during class, so they couldn't claim they didn't know when things were due.

In the lab, things were a bit more relaxed but still structured. I had one lab session every week that lasted two hours and 50 minutes, during which students conducted experiments. Some students struggled with the lack of chairs in the lab—there was no place to sit because I wanted them to get the impression, they were there to work. Lab coats were mandatory, and without one, no experiment could be done. I began each lab with a half-hour lecture, then the students worked on their experiments, which were designed to take the full two hours. Lab reports were due at the beginning of the next class, giving students a week to complete them.

I also had office hours, where students could come for advice, ask questions, or seek clarification. In addition, I attended weekly seminars, part of the university's enrichment program. I miss the quiet, still moments in my office, laboratory, and classroom before the students arrived. These spaces became like a second home to me. I miss the quick "good mornings" exchanged with colleagues in the hallway, the comforting sound of my coffee kettle hissing, and the scent of cinnamon from the tea I kept in my office. My routine even included a bag of supplies for the lab to use for experimentation.

But above all, I miss the students—their inquisitive minds and the friendships they built with each other. I always ensured the lab was clean and organized before class, taking a picture to show them how it should look after they completed their experiments. I wanted them to learn the importance of leaving the lab in the same condition they found it.

I miss the chaos and noise, the surprise acts of kindness, and those quiet, delicate moments when students from all backgrounds learned to navigate the challenges of working and learning together. In those moments, I was reminded of my role as their teacher, a role I took seriously. My job was to teach, and I did so with all the power and passion I could muster because I wanted nothing more than to see my students succeed in life.

A person does not miss what they do not know.

28. Student Success!

I've spent most of my life teaching chemistry, and over the years, I've witnessed countless student success stories. Some are particularly memorable, especially when they come full circle in unexpected ways. One of the most touching moments happened last year during the height of the pandemic. I contracted COVID-19, and although I took the necessary precautions after testing positive, it was too late for my wife, who had already been exposed. She experienced much more severe symptoms than I did, and I took care of her while seeking forgiveness, feeling guilty for unknowingly putting her at risk. I was fortunate that my symptoms were milder, but the fatigue was overwhelming—I slept for 36 hours straight. However, after three days, my symptoms persisted, and I needed to visit an urgent care facility.

The facility wasn't fully equipped to handle COVID cases, but the doctor kindly prescribed Paxlovid, an antiviral medication. I headed to the closest CVS pharmacy to get my prescription filled. When I handed my prescription to the pharmacy technician, she advised me not to take Paxlovid because, by that time, three days had already passed since I contracted the virus. She was quite firm in her recommendation and soon called the pharmacist over to discuss it further. The pharmacist was equally adamant that I shouldn't take the medication, explaining that Paxlovid might reintroduce the virus into my system and potentially prolong my illness. They made it clear that

while I had the choice to take it, their professional advice
was to refrain from doing so.

I decided to trust their guidance, and the next day, I felt
noticeably better. My throat, which had been unbearably
painful, seemed to heal almost miraculously. The following
day, I called the pharmacy to express my gratitude to the
pharmacist who had given me such sound advice. After
being on hold for a bit, I spoke to another pharmacist, and I
described the woman I had initially spoken with—a lady of
Asian descent whose country of origin I wasn't certain of.
The pharmacist promised to relay my message. Just before
we ended the call, she asked for my name. When I told her,
there was a brief pause. Then she spoke, "Dr. Moges, I was
your student five years ago at the university. I'm the
pharmacist here now, and I'm so happy that everything
worked out with the other pharmacist."

It was a touching moment of realization. I remembered
her and felt immense pride knowing that she had progressed
in her career to become a pharmacist. From that same class
of 12 students, three of them went on to become
pharmacists—a testament to their hard work and dedication.

Another success story that stands out involved a group
of pharmacy students in my instrumental analysis class. At
the end of the semester, I assigned a semester project where
I asked them to invent an instrument of their choice based
on the concepts they had learned throughout the term.
Every time I brought up the project, one inquisitive student
would repeatedly ask for clarification, as if she didn't
understand what I was asking for. This went on for several
class sessions. Finally, one of the classmates, who is now

also a pharmacist, stood up on my behalf. She expressed her frustration, telling her peers that they understood the project perfectly well, and she couldn't understand why they kept asking the same questions, as it was exhausting me.

When the time came for them to present their projects—both orally and in written form—I was truly amazed at the creativity and ingenuity they demonstrated. The instruments each group invented far exceeded my expectations. It was a proud moment to see how much they had absorbed and how they applied their knowledge. The second pharmacist from that class has since returned to speak to current STEM majors at the university, continuing the cycle of mentorship and inspiration.

One unforgettable memory occurred when I was teaching physical chemistry, specifically on the topic of alcohols. During the lesson, I casually mentioned that we should avoid drinking alcohol. One of my students became visibly upset and asked if I had ever consumed alcohol when I was younger. He angrily expressed frustration, accusing older generations of doing whatever they wanted in their youth and then imposing restrictions on younger people. That same student graduated that year, but four years later, he returned to my office to share that he had gone to medical school and was now a doctor an MD. Two years after that, he visited again to tell me he had completed his residency and had secured a job as a doctor at a hospital. He was one of the students I still remember clearly.

These stories remind me of the deep and lasting impact that teaching can have. Seeing my former students thrive in their careers, particularly in critical fields like pharmacy during such challenging times, fills me with pride and reinforces my belief in the value of education. It's moments like these that make all the effort worthwhile, knowing that the seeds I planted in the classroom have blossomed into successful and impactful careers.

You don't grab the tail of a tiger, but if you do, don't let go.

29. Teaching at a College

My experience at a nearby college is one that stands out
as both unique and unexpected, and I'd like to share it here.
At the time, I was teaching at a two-year community
college, and since it serves as a "feeder" school, four-year
colleges occasionally invited faculty from the community
college for lunch. One day, during one of these lunches,
something rather serendipitous happened. We were sitting at
the table, and one of the participants suggested that each
person introduce themselves. The woman leading this
initiative was the head of the science at the college. When it
was my turn, I introduced myself as a chemistry teacher.
Upon hearing this, she immediately perked up and told the
group that she had been desperately searching for a
chemistry instructor. In that moment, I was offered the
position as an adjunct chemistry teacher—without even
having to submit an application or go through an oral
interview! It all happened so organically. For the next six
years, I taught chemistry at the four-year college. My salary
from the community college was already sufficient to cover
all my living expenses, so the income from Barton felt like
an unexpected but much-appreciated bonus—a true "icing
on the cake."

One of my more interesting memories during my time at
college happened while I was using the gym facilities.
There's an indoor track on the second floor of the gym that
encircles the basketball court below, with the two levels
separated by a rail. I enjoyed walking around that track on
occasion, and one day, I noticed a group of ladies playing

basketball on the court below. They were lively, full of energy, and every time one of them made a basket, they'd let out loud cheers, screams, and laughter. It was clear they were having a fantastic time. This went on for a while—just an outpouring of joy and friendship.

But then, something caught my attention. After a while, they stopped playing basketball and began setting up goals on both sides of the court. It took me a moment to realize that they were preparing to play soccer. As soon as they switched from basketball to soccer, the atmosphere changed completely. The noise, the shouting, the laughter—it all stopped. Suddenly, the room became so quiet that you could hear a pin drop. They started kicking the ball, but there were no shouts of celebration or encouragement like before. The only sounds were the occasional blow of a whistle or the subtle thud of the ball being kicked. It struck me that while these same women had been exuberant and loud during their basketball game, they were professional soccer players, they were completely focused, precise, and quiet.

Watching this transformation, it dawned on me that people act differently when they are operating within their natural gifts. It was clear to me that these women were far more comfortable and skilled at soccer than basketball, and this showed in how they played. While they had fun with basketball, their real talent and passion were revealed when they played soccer. It was as if, when they stepped into their true element, their demeanor changed—they became more serious, focused, and purposeful. This experience served as a metaphor for me, illustrating how important it is to recognize and nurture our gifts and abilities. When we're operating in our true calling, everything flows more naturally, with a sense of calm and quiet confidence.

Teaching at both colleges provided not only a valuable opportunity to impart knowledge to my students but also allowed me to reflect on these important life lessons. Whether in the classroom or on the court, we can all learn something profound when we're truly in our element.

To the idle, everything seems simple.

30. Publishing in an Open Journal

Writing and speaking have long been personal challenges for me, and the process of composing this essay has been particularly demanding. After the pandemic struck, my brother encouraged me to publish something, but the task felt overwhelming. I didn't believe I could write anything worthy of publication. Writing seemed daunting, especially as I wrestled with what topic to focus on. Nonetheless, I eventually took on the challenge, and my first published paper in North Carolina was titled "Teaching Students Synthesizing Molecules Mimicking an Existing Drug Against COVID-19."

This paper was a product of the pandemic's widespread impact. It allowed me to integrate my teaching with an urgent scientific inquiry into potential treatments for COVID-19. The assignment I gave my students—to synthesize molecules mimicking existing drugs against the virus—was ambitious. While many students found it overwhelming, one student approached the project with exceptional dedication, which inspired me to write about the work she has done. Her commitment and success became a motivating force behind the completion of my first published paper.

Even though I had made the decision to write, the process remained slow and difficult. I remember sitting at my desk, struggling to find the right words. On a good day, I managed to write just a paragraph. Each sentence was a challenge, and the flow of ideas often felt blocked. Yet, I pushed through, determined to contribute to the academic discourse despite the uphill battle. Over the next four years, I managed to publish twelve papers, a feat I had never imagined possible. These accomplishments serve as a reminder that persistence, even in the face of challenges like writing, can lead to growth and success.

Among my publications, "The Alarming Toxicity of Ruta Graveolens" stands out as the most-referred paper, having garnered hundreds of citations. Ruta graveolens, commonly known as rue, has a long history in traditional medicine, but my research brought to light its toxic properties, particularly when used without medical supervision. This work underscored the risks associated with using certain medicinal plants, prompting a reevaluation of their safety and guiding both researchers and practitioners toward more informed usage. The referrals to this paper indicate its significant contribution to the field of toxicology and pharmacology.

Moreover, through these papers, I was able to recognize and give credit to my traditional as well as early college students who had contributed to the research. Without our help many of these students would not publish before or after receiving their degrees, an achievement that I believe significantly advanced their academic careers. This recognition also fostered a culture of early involvement in research, which I consider one of my most significant accomplishments. In a scientific community where the pressure to "publish or perish" is prevalent, I feel that my efforts have added real value.

Teaching during the pandemic also prompted innovative approaches, such as the use of virtual laboratory platforms to teach key concepts, like human buffer solutions and drug synthesis. This shift required adaptability, much like I had to adapt my approach to writing and publishing. The combination of academic rigor and practical applications in this period highlights the importance of evolving in response to challenges.

The pencil leaves marks where it's pressed.

31. Reverse Planning

I wish I had known about reverse planning when I was younger. Reverse planning is a method that involves beginning with the desired outcome and then working backward to determine the steps necessary to achieve that outcome. It's a strategy often used in project management and education but has powerful implications for personal life planning as well. By visualizing the end goal first, you gain a clear sense of purpose and direction, which helps guide decisions and actions along the way.

One of the biggest advantages of reverse planning is that it allows us to map out our life goals and create a timeline for achieving them. This is especially relevant for people over forty who may be facing a midlife crisis, unsure of how to plan the rest of their lives. For many young people, thinking about their future in such long-term increments seems unnecessary, or even overwhelming. When I was in my twenties and thirties, the age of forty seemed so distant—an age where I thought it would be too late to start anything new. But looking back now, I realize that reverse planning could have helped me navigate the uncertainties of my early life and career with greater clarity.

For example, I was 47 when my youngest son was born, which may seem late by many people's standards. Now, years later, I have watched him graduate with double majors in electrical and computer engineering and complete his master's in engineering. As an immigrant from Ethiopia, I started my family later than many people do. I was 28 when I finished my education and began settling into life, and it wasn't until I was 34 that I got married to my wife, Tenu. My first son was born when I was 37, and I welcomed my grandchildren in my late 60s. I advised my friends and family to marry earlier, from my experience, but my path was different. Had I embraced reverse planning sooner, perhaps I would have made different decisions about timing, but I ultimately followed the course that felt right for me.

Reverse planning can be particularly helpful for younger generations who are just starting their adult lives. For instance, I've taught reverse planning as part of an introductory course for first-year college students. I would begin by asking them to think about when they want to become a grandparent. If they want to be a grandparent by the age of 60, they must plan their life accordingly. Typically, it takes about 25 years for children to grow up, finish school, get married, and have their own children. If students want to reach grandparenthood by 60, they must be parents by 35, which means they should finish their education, get married, and have children within a specific timeframe.

When I teach the principle of reverse planning, I have the kids line up from youngest to oldest and ask each one to share what they're currently learning, like reading, writing, or multiplication tables, up to the more advanced skills of teenagers and college students. Then, I go back to the beginning and ask them if they aim to graduate from high school at seventeen. From there, I guide them to think about what they need to achieve at each age to reach that goal.

In some cultures, like in India and other parts of Asia, people often finish having children by their late twenties. If my students express a desire to be great-grandparents by the age of seventy, by the age ten years they should marry and have children—which is impossible to do. This kind of reverse planning encouraged my students to think critically about their long-term goals, how their personal and professional choices align with those goals, and what steps they need to take now to stay on course. Although reverse planning has both pros and cons, I believe its benefits far outweigh the challenges, especially when it helps individuals avoid unnecessary stress later in life.

One critical precaution I emphasize is the potential consequences of having children before getting married. Early parenthood, especially when unplanned, can introduce several complications. It often leads to quitting school, juggling child support, and delays in achieving other life goals. These challenges can create long-term effects, hindering personal and professional development. By reverse planning, students can better understand how their small choices today impact their future and plan more strategically to reach their desired milestones.

In event planning, political campaigns, and major life events, reverse planning has proven to be an invaluable tool. By keeping the end goal in mind, people can anticipate obstacles, map out strategies, and make more informed decisions that lead them closer to their desired outcomes. Looking back, I wish I had learned this principle earlier in life. It's something that could benefit anyone, especially young people, by helping them set and achieve goals with greater purpose and intention.

Shallow attempts don't reach the depth needed.

32. We Need Each Other!

In life, no matter how independent or self-reliant one may feel, the presence and support of others—family, friends, or colleagues—become essential, especially during pivotal moments of joy and sorrow. While I tend to be shy and prefer to navigate life alone, I recognize that the company of loved ones is indispensable. Human connection is a powerful source of strength and encouragement.

This reminds me of a story from one of my colleagues about his experience at a previous job. He was responsible for many critical tasks, including managing purchases, and he noticed that several of his coworkers were periodically recognized with awards for their service. After years of dedication, he realized that he had never received any recognition. Feeling overlooked, he approached his boss and asked why he hadn't been acknowledged like the others. His boss, surprised, responded by reminding him that he had access to the company credit card and could easily buy himself any plaques and gifts he wished. But for my colleague, it wasn't about the physical object or the ability to purchase recognition—it was the act of being acknowledged by others that held true value. He longed for the validation that comes from being seen and appreciated by those around him, not just a token he could buy for himself.

When I was in graduate school, I worked tirelessly to get through my coursework so I could dedicate more time to my research. After four years of intense effort, the moment of graduation finally arrived. But something felt incomplete—I had no family or friends to invite, no one to share the joy of this significant achievement with. Without anyone to celebrate with, I couldn't find the motivation to participate in the ceremony. I didn't buy the cap and gown, I skipped the rehearsal, and opted out of the graduation festivities altogether. In the absence of loved ones to share that moment, the achievement felt hollow, and I didn't see the need to go through the motions of celebration. However, many years later, when I earned my master's degree in divinity, the situation was drastically different. By this time, I was married, had four children, and we hosted a house church in our home. On top of that, we had a large network of relatives living nearby in the Washington, D.C. area. They all came together to celebrate my graduation, and the experience was filled with joy. Over 100 people attended the graduation party, and one of our dear friends baked twelve different cakes for the event. Despite the long journey for some of the attendees, they made sacrifices to be there. We rented a hall with a kitchen, and it became a major celebration. In comparison to my Ph.D. graduation, this one—while a lower degree—felt so much more fulfilling. The presence of family and friends made all the difference.

This idea was further driven home by a story one of my friends shared. He was hired as an engineer and was excited to start his new job. On his first day, he organized his office and set up his workspace, complete with a computer and a phone. The second day was spent sorting out HR paperwork. However, as the days went by, he began to feel idle, unsure of what he was supposed to do. Despite attending meetings getting his paychecks, he felt increasingly disconnected from his role. Eventually, he reached out to one of the senior workers in the manufacturing plant, explaining that no one had told him what his responsibilities were. The worker, surprised, apologized and explained that everyone assumed he knew what to do. His role, as it turned out, was to identify and resolve any engineering issues in the plant.

This experience reinforced an essential lesson: we need each other, not just for guidance but for clarity and direction. Even in professional settings, where we might expect independence, the reality is that collaboration, communication, and mutual support are necessary. Just as my friend needed someone to clarify his job responsibilities, we all need others to help us navigate our paths, whether in work, life, or celebration.

Just as the eye is sensitive to touch, those who love you are sensitive to your pain.

33. Starting a Church

Starting a church can be incredibly fulfilling but also laden with challenges, many of which are not apparent at first glance. My journey into ministry was not a straight path, nor was it easy. Before I embarked on this endeavor, I was managing a successful orphanage in Ethiopia. My role focused primarily on raising funds, and while that was crucial, I felt an internal call to serve as the spiritual leader for the children and staff. Realizing that this required a deeper theological foundation, I decided to pursue seminary education. I registered for classes at a university divinity school and ultimately completed my master's degree at another seminary.

Despite fulfilling the academic requirements, nothing could have fully prepared me for the challenges of pastoring a church. The first church we started gathered at a university's chapel, with our meetings held every Sunday at 3:00 PM, followed by dinner prepared by my wife, Tenu, and my mother-in-law. Even though I had the theological knowledge, the actual work of pastoring was a learning experience. Each Sunday, I stood before a diverse congregation with a mix of backgrounds, including a significant group of Ethiopian Orthodox Christians who attended our church for about a year. I dedicated myself to preaching evangelistic sermons, hoping to guide the congregation towards conversion but they eventually decided to open their own Orthodox church.

In the meantime, my family played a critical role in our church services. My eldest son played the keyboard, my daughter led the singing, and my younger son played the drums, with my youngest learning from his siblings. My wife and a few other women formed the choir and helped lead the church as elders. The congregation was filled with people who brought their unique stories, like Eddie who was homeless but shared compelling testimonies of his faith journey. One church member, gifted in preaching and teaching, was eventually ordained and opened his own church. There were also moments of joy, such as officiating weddings and baptisms for church members who became lifelong friends. I met an acquaintance at a wedding, and he reminded me that I was the one who baptized him at the church.

But pastoring is not as glamorous as it might seem. Our church's beginnings were bittersweet, as we had to leave another congregation. This separation caused deep emotional wounds, and when new members decided to leave, we also felt abandoned and rejected. There were other sacrifices along the way. For a while, we had to rent and hold services at a park, where we carried all our musical instruments and equipment each week, setting up and dismantling before and after every service. This physical labor, coupled with the emotional highs and lows of ministry, often left us feeling worn out. Yet, these trials were an integral part of earning our place in ministry. Thankfully, we had purchased a home, which, with the help of the congregation, we converted into a functional and welcoming house church.

Through it all, the rewards were immense: baptizing many into the faith, officiating weddings, and watching our children grow in their Christian faith and take on leadership roles in the church. Our success stories—a congregation of committed believers, spiritual growth within my own family, and the countless lives touched by our ministry— serve as a testament to the power of perseverance and faith in the pastoral calling. The challenges were real, but the rewards were far greater.

It is unrealistic kneading before grinding.

34. The Challenges of Marriage

Marriage can be a rewarding journey, but it's also filled with challenges that test a couple's commitment. When I was interning as a chaplain at a medical center nearly 20% of people never marry in their lives, and they never experience what surviving the many ups and downs of marriage—whether financial, emotional, physical, social, or spiritual achievement. I got married in my 30s, and four decades later, I'm still benefiting from the deep connection marriage offers. One of the greatest gifts has been emotional intimacy, providing me with shared life's joys and hardships with Tenu. This companionship has helped reduce feelings of loneliness, increased my happiness, and given me a greater sense of purpose. Beyond emotional support, marriage has positively impacted my overall health. Married people, including myself, tend to adopt healthier lifestyles—avoiding harmful habits, exercising regularly, and taking care of each other's well-being.

Despite these benefits, marriage doesn't come without its difficulties. Financial stress, emotional disconnect, and the complexities of living closely with someone else can challenge even the strongest relationships. Tragically, some couples experience devastating outcomes. I recall last week's story of a Kenyan gold medal runner who was tragically killed by her ex-boyfriend and who also died a few days later, illustrating how love can sometimes turn into pain. There are couples I have married that fell apart due to difficult circumstances. One couple divorced after the husband lost a leg to gangrene, and the wife decided she still wanted to go out to clubs and dance. Another marriage crumbled after the wife stole from her mother-in-law, destroying the husband's trust. These real-life examples show that marriages can falter for many reasons, sometimes despite love and commitment. Other marriages have blossomed with beautiful children and successful couples.

What has helped me navigate these challenges is the realization that while problems may take on different forms, they are often fundamentally the same. As a father, I hope to offer my children and grandchildren the wisdom gained from my own experiences to help them navigate the same struggles in their marriages. The lessons learned in one generation can serve as valuable advice for the next.

Understanding that each spouse comes from a unique background, with different life experiences and perspectives, is essential to a successful marriage. In premarital counseling, I emphasize the importance of recognizing these differences and treating each other with respect, acknowledging that both partners are made in the image of God. I also advise couples to engage in honest, blame-free communication and encourage them to seek support from friends, family, and their faith community. Participating in social and church groups can provide much-needed support and strengthen the bond between spouses.

The daily routines in marriage—like eating meals together or planning family activities—can sometimes feel mundane, but they are opportunities to foster deeper connections. Finding ways to resolve conflicts in a healthy, respectful manner is essential to maintaining a strong marriage. Self-care is equally important. Looking after our physical health, dressing well, and maintaining a clean home all contribute to a happier, more fulfilling relationship. One of my favorite examples comes from my seminary professor, who, after arguments with his wife, would reward himself with an ice cream cone—the size depending on the severity of the disagreement—while his wife found peace tending to her garden. These small rituals can help couples deal with the inevitable ups and downs of marriage, offering comfort and perspective during difficult times.

If you take care of your wife when she is young, she will take care of you when you are old.

35. Show Time

This morning, while I was in the locker room at the gym, I overheard a conversation between two members. The facility offers water aerobics classes, creatively named "H$_2$O aerobics." Initially, I assumed it was simply an exercise class for the elderly to help maintain joint mobility, especially since the average participant appeared to be well over seventy. However, after attending a few sessions myself, I now fully appreciate the value and enjoyment these classes offer.

As I listened, the first gentleman asked, "How are you doing?" The second man responded with a resigned sigh, "I'm dealing with the usual old age issues," and proceeded to list the aches and pains that had become a part of his daily life. The first man, clearly sympathetic, said, "I was looking forward to old age. I'm sorry to hear about all the problems it brings." The second man tried to reverse his complaints, attempting to put a more positive spin on things, but the damage had already been done. His initial lament was hard to take back, and the realities of aging hung in the air.

Their exchange got me thinking about the various stages of life and the moments when we are called to perform, to act, to show up—whether we feel ready or not. For media personalities, "show time" means stepping into the spotlight and delivering with precision and flair. As a teacher, my "show time" was when the clock struck, and the classroom came alive with eager (or sometimes reluctant) students waiting for me to deliver my lecture. In scientific research, the countdown to an experiment often felt like the final seconds before a performance, and by 1 o'clock, it was "experiment time." Some of my students were athletes, particularly those in team sports, experienced this when game begins—their skills, preparation, and endurance are all put on display.

Now, here I am, three months into my retirement, and it's "show time" in a whole new way. Retirement isn't the end of productivity; it's the start of a new chapter. It's time for me to reinvent my daily routine—transforming the structured eight-to-five workday into something equally meaningful, something that will still allow me to contribute and grow.

Every action I take now feels like a performance, a deliberate move to stay engaged and present in life. Whether I'm exercising, teaching Sunday school, working in the yard, or even writing this essay—it's all "show time." Nothing I do is trivial; everything has a purpose. I've come to embrace the rhythm of life's stages: conception, where I was nurtured in my mother's womb; infancy, where I was tenderly cared for; childhood, marked by discovery and education; adolescence, full of the trials and monotony of growing up; my twenties and thirties, a time of significant decisions that shaped the path ahead; midlife, when energy wanes but wisdom grows; and now, old age, with its freedoms and limitations. Eventually, I'll reach the final stage—when it all ends—but until then, I want to make every day count!

To make a difference in life, I need to keep striving and remain creative. This isn't the time to slow down or succumb to complacency. Life is moving forward, and I'm still in the game. Sometimes I look at all the incredible inventions around me—from the cars I drive, to the hot water heaters that bring comfort, to the jacuzzi at the center where I relax, and even the seasonal clothes that keep me warm in the winter or cool in the summer. These are all the results of someone's vision and effort. They seized their moment. Now, it's my turn. I must seize mine. It's the big moment, my time to act—my "show time."

If a hamburger isn't flipped, it will burn.

36. Sharing Grief and Loss with a Neighbor

This afternoon, we faced one of the most difficult tasks imaginable: informing our neighbor of the passing of his mother, who lived in Ethiopia while battling cancer for many years. Despite her long fight, undergoing rounds of chemotherapy, the news was devastating. Of all the things I've done in my life, this was perhaps the hardest. Even thinking about it now makes me feel sick to my stomach.

In our culture, it's customary to gather friends and family to share the news. This allows the grieving process to begin with the support of loved ones. We gathered in the living room of his house at exactly 1:44 PM. It was just four of his close friends, my spouse Tenu and I, all of us sitting in silence, waiting for him to arrive. A close friend had taken him out for a short while, and during that time, the tension in the room was almost unbearable. The stress was so thick, it felt as if you could cut it with a knife.

As we waited, I couldn't help but recall another painful memory—when one of my cousins was informed of his father's passing. He had been away in Europe on a scholarship, and by the time he returned, his father had already passed. I remember vividly how he reacted to the news—he ran straight into the woods in shock and grief. Thankfully, a relative followed him and brought him back safely, but it was a reminder of how unpredictable grief can be.

Finally, the moment came. When our neighbor arrived with his friend, it seemed he already suspected the worst. He hesitated at the door, reluctant to come in. Our hearts were pounding, worried about how he would react. We were especially concerned for his safety, watching carefully to ensure he wouldn't hurt himself in his grief. After a few moments of hesitation, he came inside, and the moment he stepped through the door, the tears began. His cries echoed through the room, a raw, painful sound that broke the silence we had been sitting in for what felt like an eternity.

For the next hour, the house was filled with silence, punctuated only by his occasional sobs. By that time, more people had arrived to offer their support—about ten of us in total. You could have heard a pin drop in that room, the weight of grief so heavy that words felt unnecessary.

Wanting to offer some comfort, we decided to serve food. We organized with the rest of his friends to order from a nearby restaurant, providing a variety of dishes. Tenu and our neighbor took it upon themselves to serve the food, along with coffee and tea. Although the atmosphere was somber, sharing a meal together was a small way of showing that we were there for him, united in grief and support during this painful time.

As the day ended, the sadness and sense of loss hung in the air, reminding us how fragile life is. Even though we tried our best to support him, nothing could take away his deep pain. Seeing him break down and hearing his heartbreaking cries showed how much it hurts when we lose someone we love. But in the silence and tears, there was some comfort in just being there together. By serving food, offering tea, and sitting quietly, we gave more than words ever could—our presence, love, and the assurance that he wasn't alone in his hardest moment. Sometimes, that small bit of support is all we can give.

Loving and losing is better than never loving at all.

37. Lessons from Heartfelt Generosity

One of the most important lessons I've always wanted to teach is the value of giving. While many people are quick to receive, few have a natural inclination toward giving. We see this even in the political arena, where candidates often make grand promises of giving back to the people, but once in office, they tend to take more than they give. This attitude isn't limited to politics—it's visible in the business world as well. Many CEOs and leaders work relentlessly to climb the ladder of success. They understand what it feels like to lack resources, to go hungry for both material things and opportunities. But when they reach the top, many forget the very communities they came from. They forget the simple truth: it is better to give than to receive.

There's a beautiful promise in the Bible about giving: "Give, and it will be given to you. A good measure, pressed down, shaken together, and running over, will be poured into your lap. For with the measure you use, it will be measured to you." This principle is often overlooked by those who, once they've achieved success, become focused on keeping what they have rather than sharing it with others.

Growing up in Ethiopia, I was part of a culture that truly lived by the desire to give. Hospitality was not a formality; it was a way of life. In the past people could travel from one end of the country to the other without food or drink because residents welcomed travelers with open arms. They would provide food, water, and even their own beds to ensure people were comfortable. I remember guests coming to our home, and how my great-grandmother would prepare food for them right in front of their eyes, using a small charcoal stove. Guests never left our house without being offered a meal. As children, we would compete for the chance to serve our guests, whether it was pouring water for them to wash their hands or even helping them wash their feet.

The joy of giving was ingrained in us from a young age, and it was never about material wealth. It was about the pride of serving, of showing respect and love to others. That same spirit of generosity is something I try to instill in the children I teach in Sunday school. I encourage them to share their toys and help them understand that giving is not just about material things—it's about sharing joy, time, and kindness. During Christmas, I give each child a card with a twenty-dollar bill and their picture on a card, teaching them that the act of giving, no matter how small, can bring great joy. My Sunday school lessons are meant to resonate not only with the kids but also with the teenagers, parents, and grandparents who are listening. The hope is to plant the seeds of generosity in their hearts so that they grow up understanding the true value of giving.

However, not everyone sees the beauty in giving. A friend once told me, "If we both have $100, and you ask to borrow $25, and I give it to you, now you have $125, and I'm left with only $75. That's why I don't like to give." This mindset is, unfortunately, all too common. People often focus on what they're losing instead of recognizing the potential for joy and fulfillment that comes from giving.

But giving, in its truest form, enriches both the giver and the receiver.

Another heartwarming example of the joy of giving involves a mother who found great happiness in seeing her husband receive all the credit for raising their daughter. When the girl was young and living in Ethiopia, she suffered a terrible accident on a railroad track and lost both of her legs. She was sent to an orphanage where, due to her disability, she remained for a long time—no one wanted to adopt her. Then, one day, a couple from the United States came to the orphanage looking to adopt a child. Despite the director's recommendation to choose another child, the couple fell in love with this little girl and adopted her, bringing her home to America.

As the years passed, the girl flourished in her new environment. She excelled in school and even in sports, overcoming her physical challenges. Her story became so inspiring that she was invited for an interview on a television show. During the interview, they asked the girl how she learned to swim, and she proudly explained how her father had taken the time to teach her, step by step. When asked about her academic success, the girl shared how her dad would pick her up from school every day and tutor her until she understood her lessons. Throughout the interview, the mother sat on stage, beaming with pride, as her daughter continually praised her husband. Even though they tried to shift the spotlight to the mother, the daughter remained focused on how much her father had helped her. The mother, far from being upset by the lack of recognition, was overjoyed. Her happiness didn't come from receiving credit, but from knowing that her daughter was thriving and happy. She embodied the essence of selfless giving—finding joy in the success of others.

Giving is like lending to the Lord, and no one who gives ever loses.

38. Exploring Herbal Chemistry: Engaging Students Through Nature's Lab

Teaching and learning lessons from herbal chemistry offer a rich and engaging framework that captivates students' interests while grounding them in scientific principles. The introduction to herbal chemistry underscores the importance of herbal plants as safe, natural sources of chemicals that can be effectively utilized in a variety of experiments. This perspective encourages students to explore and discuss common herbs they encounter in their everyday lives, such as basil, mint, and garden cress, highlighting their potential scientific applications.

In hands-on experimentation, students can immerse themselves in the world of herbs, identifying different plant parts—roots, stems, leaves, flowers—and examining their distinctive smells and textures. This sensory exploration links experiential learning to scientific inquiry, making abstract concepts more tangible. By focusing on garden cress, for example, students not only learned about its health benefits and nutritional value but also engage in discussions about its traditional medicinal uses. This fosters a deeper understanding of cultural significance and encourages students to undertake research projects that connect scientific learning with cultural contexts.

Additionally, students can investigate using acid-base titration experiments with garden cress. By observing color changes to determine pH levels, they can explore how anthocyanins—natural pigments found in the plant—affect color. The extraction of phytochemicals from garden cress can also be demonstrated using powdered seeds and various solvents. Students will learn to calculate yields, assess extraction efficiency, and understand the practical applications of their findings.

Testing the antimicrobial properties of garden cress using the Kirby-Bauer method provided another avenue for inquiry. Students compared their results with a control substance like penicillin, leading to discussions about the role of herbal medicine in contemporary healthcare practices. This process not only sharpened their analytical skills but also fostered an appreciation for the potential of herbal remedies.

Moreover, these experiments are designed to be budget-friendly, addressing the financial constraints that many schools face. By utilizing commonly available herbs, educators can significantly reduce lab costs while still providing effective and meaningful learning opportunities. In conclusion, this approach emphasizes that innovative methods of extraction and testing can enrich the educational experience while minimizing the use of toxic chemicals. It encourages educators to explore further ways of incorporating natural materials into science lessons, igniting curiosity and inspiring future scientific inquiries.

Ants don't possess shovels, and flies don't have places to live.

39. A Sermon Never Preached!

When a person loses a loved one, it's not just the weight of grief that they bear, but also the emotional and physical exhaustion that comes with such a profound loss. In these moments, friends, and family gather, bound by compassion and empathy, to offer their support. Some travel long distances, while others are local, but regardless of where they come from, everyone comes together to ease the burden of grief. One tangible way they show their care is by bringing cooked food and drinks, relieving the mourning family of the need to prepare meals for the many guests. It's a simple, yet profound act of kindness—one that says, "You are not alone in this." During this gathering, I prepared a sermon, hoping to offer not just spiritual guidance, but also empathy and hope for those grappling with loss.

Grieving families often wrestle with feelings of abandonment, questioning, "Where is God in all this suffering?" and "If He truly is in control, why did He allow this to happen?" These deeply personal and painful questions have echoed through the hearts of many for centuries. I recall, many years ago, witnessing a student crossing the college quad, his voice raw with emotion as he grappled with the same question. He asked, "Is God anywhere?" and, answering himself with a voice that vibrated through the air, he declared, "He is nowhere." His words carried the weight of his anguish, reflecting a deep sense of disbelief in God, a sentiment that resonated with others who were perhaps wrestling with their own feelings of doubt.

This profound sense of despair is something we can all empathize with, as suffering often obscures our ability to see beyond the pain. But just because we can't see something doesn't mean it doesn't exist. In life, there are many things we cannot see—thoughts, emotions, love, fear, and joy. These unseen forces shape our experiences, guide our actions, and influence the world around us, even though they are invisible to the eye. In a similar way, though we may not see God physically, His presence and care are often felt in the quiet moments of comfort, in the kindness of others, and in the love that surrounds us during our darkest hours.

In the Christian faith, we believe that God's love for humanity was made tangible through the life of His Son, Jesus Christ. Jesus came to teach, heal, and cast out demons, showing us that God not only exists but is deeply invested in our well-being. Through His name, Christians are empowered to carry on His work, offering healing, comfort, and empathy to those in need. Another important truth to remember is that whatever happened to Jesus—His suffering and eventual death—may also happen to us as His followers. He lived a human life, experienced deep suffering, and ultimately died. As we follow in His footsteps, we too are bound to encounter the pain and trials that life brings. Yet, we are not alone in these experiences.

I wanted to share this profound comfort in knowing that God is with us in our suffering. Psalm 34:15 offers words of consolation, reminding us, "The eyes of the Lord are on the righteous, and His ears are attentive to their cry; the Lord is close to the brokenhearted and saves those who are crushed in spirit." This promise assures us that God is not distant, but near—especially in moments when we feel most broken.

I also wanted to share my journey to faith in Christ which came after years of studying and teaching various religions. What set Christianity apart for me was its portrayal of a God who actively demonstrates love, forgiveness, and salvation. In many other belief systems, salvation depends on an individual's ability to perform good deeds or follow specific practices. However, in Christianity, it is not our efforts that save us, but God's unconditional love and grace freely given to us.

During this time of mourning, I found myself reflecting on these comforting truths. Even though we may never fully understand why suffering happens, I tried to reassure the family that God is present in our pain. While I didn't preach this message at the time, it has stayed in my heart that God knows our struggles and cares deeply when we are brokenhearted. With the support of faith, family, and friends, I hope they find solace in knowing that, even in the hardest moments, they are never alone.

A gun without a bullet is a stick incapable of fulfilling its intended purpose.

40. Baptism

The day was approaching when my first son and my daughter get baptized. It was at the historic chapel at Saint Augustine University and the priest has given us space to meet at the church for our weekly service. The first challenge was ensuring that the baptism pool could hold water—a task that turned out to be far more difficult than I had anticipated. I wasn't a mason by any means, but there I was, buying bags of cement, carefully filling in the cracks and sealing the holes, all in the hope that the water would stay where it was supposed to.

At one point, my brother-in-law, who had been observing my struggle, couldn't help but make a remark. With a grin on his face, he said, "If you've spent as much time on your sermon as you did with that pool, it would probably be the greatest sermon ever preached." His words hit me with a mix of humor and truth. I laughed it off, but deep down I knew that he had a point. I was so caught up in the physical task at hand that I hadn't given the same attention to the spiritual preparation I was supposed to be leading. The irony wasn't lost on me—the work of fixing the pool seemed almost symbolic of the deeper work I needed to do within myself, ensuring that I was ready not just to perform a baptism, but to deliver a message that could resonate with people's hearts.

The next step in preparing for the event was to invite guests, a task my wife took on with a determination that left me both amazed and grateful. From the beginning, she had challenged me with a promise: as long as I focused on attending seminary and learning how to preach, she would fill the church with people. True to her word, she set to work, reaching out to families and friends, not just locally but from as far as the Research Triangle, Washington, D.C., and even Richmond. Her dedication to ensuring the church was filled with guests was unwavering, and it gave me the confidence to focus fully on crafting a sermon that would live up to the occasion.

On the day of the event, her efforts paid off in ways I could have only imagined. The church was packed with people, and my sermon, thanks to both my preparation and the supportive atmosphere, was one of the best I had ever delivered. Professional singers graced the service, filling the space with beautiful melodies that elevated the entire experience. But the highlight of the day was the baptism itself. Two children, along with a third individual, were baptized, and each of them shared their heartfelt testimonies, touching everyone in attendance. Their stories of faith and transformation added a deeply personal and spiritual dimension to the celebration. The day was rounded off with a feast that was as excellent as the service itself—delicious food, beautifully presented, with everything going off without a hitch. It was a day where everything seemed to come together perfectly, a true reflection of both my wife and her mother's tireless efforts and the grace that carried us through each step of the journey.

Parents blessing is a lifetime protection.

41. Transforming Potential: From Struggle to Success!

Many of the people who were coming to the soup kitchen were bright with many potentials—individuals whose minds yearn to be set free. Many people have expressed to me the desire to avoid destructive lifestyle, find better jobs, quit smoking, stop drinking, or break free from drug use and other harmful habits. Yet, despite these intentions, many find themselves trapped in cycles of addiction and hopelessness, feeling ineffective in their efforts to change. This stagnation isn't due to a lack of knowledge about how to make these changes; in fact, many are aware of the steps they need to take. With countless resources available—motivational videos on YouTube, support groups, and self-help books—the real challenge lies in their inability to translate knowledge into action.

Consider the world of drug dealers. Those who navigate the complexities of chemistry to produce and distribute drugs possess valuable skills that could be redirected toward a legitimate career as chemists in pharmaceutical companies. With the right training and mentorship, they could apply their understanding of chemical reactions and substances in a way that benefits society rather than harms it.

Similarly, individuals who have engaged in sex work often develop strong emotional intelligence and empathy. These qualities could pave the way for fulfilling careers as psychologists or counselors, where they can provide support to those in need, drawing from their own experiences to foster healing and understanding.

Even those with a history of theft possess insights that could be transformative. They have a keen understanding of security and risk, which can be channeled into roles such as security advisors or advocates for community safety programs. By educating others on self-protection and the importance of community vigilance, they can help create safer environments while seeking redemption for their past choices.

Some of the homeless people have a long list of offenses for some of which they were incarcerated; they can advocate for criminal justice reform, using their stories to raise awareness about systemic issues and assist others in successfully reintegrating into society. A former runaway who found their way back can mentor at-risk youth, providing guidance based on their own experiences of hardship and resilience. Additionally, someone who has faced exploitation in the workforce can become a labor organizer, fighting for workers' rights and better conditions, utilizing their firsthand knowledge of the challenges faced by vulnerable workers.

Over time at the soup kitchen, I've witnessed incredible transformations. I've seen one person become flight instructors, others licensed truck drivers, and fire damage repair experts. I've watched some graduate from community colleges, and others who once lived in the woods now proudly rent an apartment, own a home or work full-time at different companies. These changes have shown me the power of resilience and hope, reminding me that

with the right support, anyone can turn their life around.
These stories illustrate the incredible potential that exists
within those who have faced adversity, reminding us that
change is not only possible but can lead to extraordinary
outcomes.

A deer with big horns is limited from narrow places.

42. Acceptance

I watched a political debate last night where candidates often used antagonism to reveal their opponents' weaknesses. In this debate, one candidate was consistently on the defensive while his opponent pressed sensitive issues, forcing him to respond. This pattern is familiar—when someone is challenged, their true character often comes to light. A study from the University of Missouri showed how political debates sway public opinion, especially when a candidate can hold their ground under pressure. Observing someone navigate tough moments reveals their leadership potential.

This idea of testing under pressure also connects to painful historical realities. Slave traders would intentionally antagonize enslaved individuals, putting them through grueling tests to see if they could endure harsh conditions. It's heartbreaking, but it highlights how power dynamics can strip people of their dignity. Whether in politics, history, or personal life, pressure testing reveals character.

I've seen this within my own family. Siblings and spouses often push each other's buttons, testing emotional boundaries. Antagonistic behavior, especially between siblings, establishes dominance and tests resilience. I've witnessed this with my own children and even in my marriage. Conflict can be uncomfortable, but it often reveals what lies beneath the surface—love, commitment, or unresolved issues.

Another personal experience comes to mind: when I used to cut my boys' hair myself. Out of necessity, I relied on a pair of number two clippers, and although I wasn't trained, it got the job done. The boys didn't seem to mind. Eventually, they became curious and wanted to cut each other's hair, experimenting with grading, and shaping around the edges, demonstrating a willingness to learn and improve.

When my brother-in-law migrated from Ethiopia, he took over the haircuts. As the saying goes, "It takes a village to raise a child." He was a barber and passed down his skills, teaching the boys how to properly cut and style each other's hair. Later, when they started earning stipends, they decided it was time for professional cuts and began visiting a local barber. As they grew older, they sought a different level of care and precision, reminding me of the saying, "You get what you pay for."

Both the political candidates and my boys desired to look good and gain acceptance. Everyone wants to present themselves well and avoid being exposed for their weaknesses. Bullies know how to press sensitive buttons and reveal a lack of self-confidence. The candidates aimed to earn the trust and votes of their audience, while my boys wanted to look sharp and be accepted by family, friends, and schoolmates. Just as political debates reveal character under pressure, the journey of learning to cut hair reflects a desire for growth, skill, and acceptance in the eyes of others.

A cunning fox disguises itself as holy to prey among the sheep.

43. The End

How do I write a strong and satisfying ending for my
book? One place to start is by thinking about regret.
Research shows that people often regret what they didn't
do—the missed opportunities and moments they let slip
away. I find myself reflecting on what I could have done
differently. I realize now that I didn't spend enough time
with Tenu and our family. The time we could have shared,
the words I didn't say, and the memories we didn't make
stay on my mind. I regret not working harder, not pushing
my career further, not taking care of my health, and not
making time for self-reflection. These regrets remind me
that the most important things are the people I love and my
personal growth, both spiritually and physically.

As the head of my family, I've always felt a deep sense
of responsibility. My children look to me for leadership,
expecting me to set an example for them. I've always aimed
to lead by creating meaningful experiences and traditions
for them to follow, and more importantly, to inspire them to
find their own paths. I'm reminded of a student who once
came late to class and wanted to leave early. I told him that
as a junior, he needed to set an example for the younger
students. In life, we are often put in positions of leadership,
even when we don't realize it; people look to us to rise to
the challenge!

There was a time when Tenu and I truly felt like death
was near, hovering over us like a shadow. That feeling
eventually passed, but it made the saying "life is short" very
real to me. Now, I'm reminded not to waste any time. When

I hear people say they are "killing time," I wish I could ask
them to give that time to me. Still, when I find myself being
unproductive, I feel like Gehazi, the servant of Elisha, who
traded something priceless—his integrity—for temporary
gains. I wonder if I, too, have compromised things of great
value in pursuit of fleeting rewards. There are no true
victories when we sacrifice our principles. As more of my
loved ones pass on, I look toward heaven more often,
knowing that one day, I'll arrive at my eternal destination as
well.

Two homeless veterans I've gotten to know well have
faced very different outcomes. Both have access to the
privileges and benefits that come with being a veteran. One
day, while we were discussing health, one of them told me
that when his time comes, he plans to go to the veteran's
hospital to die. The second veteran, who has kidney failure,
had been doing well for the past twelve years. We had
prayed for him, and he managed to improve his situation—
he was living in the woods but eventually got some money
and started enjoying life. However, he hasn't been taking
care of himself, and his friend told me that he likely won't
live much longer. Meanwhile, a third veteran, who had a
blocked artery, was hospitalized, and underwent surgery on
the same day. He's now doing well.

*Bankruptcy and prosperity are just a step apart, like the kitchen and
living room.*

44. The Three Pillars of a Purposeful Life: Love for God, Others, and Self

This is the driving force that gives my existence its true purpose. Three guiding principles motivate me every day: loving God, loving others, and loving myself. These cornerstones form the foundation of a life filled with meaning, peace, and connection. Loving God provides a profound sense of purpose and direction, shaping our identity and guiding our choices with wisdom and grace. It anchors us in hope and aligns our hearts with a higher calling. Loving others opens us to the beauty of compassion and the transformative power of kindness. It builds bridges of trust and community, fostering relationships that strengthen and inspire us in life's journey. Equally vital, loving yourself unlocks the door to your fullest potential. By embracing your inherent worth, healing from past wounds, and nurturing self-confidence, you empower yourself to grow and thrive.

Loving God is the cornerstone of a meaningful life. For me, it begins with daily communion through prayer—expressing gratitude, worshiping Him, and sharing my needs. As part of my New Year's resolution, I've committed to starting and ending each day in prayer, grounding my life in His presence. Over the years, reading the Bible has brought immense joy and wisdom. I'm excited about purchasing a new Bible and journeying through it from Genesis to Revelation, immersing myself in every detail, including the maps and introductions. I've discovered that reading just four chapters a day allows me to complete the entire 1,189 chapters in a year—a practice that enriches my spiritual understanding.

Teaching Sunday school has also deepened my connection to God's Word, allowing me to reflect and meditate more intentionally. Obeying His commandments is another way I strive to demonstrate my love for Him. Although returning to in-person church services after the pandemic was initially challenging, it has been a refreshing and strengthening experience, reminding me of the vital role fellowship plays in worship and dependence on God. Each day, I seek His forgiveness and renewal, trusting in His transformative work in my life.

Loving my neighbor as myself has always guided both my teaching and personal life. In the classroom, I treated my students with the same respect and care I would desire for myself. One of the simplest yet most meaningful ways I demonstrated this was by learning their names within the first two weeks of class. Although it seemed like a small gesture, remembering over sixty new students' names each year was a challenging but deeply fulfilling commitment. It acknowledged each student's individuality and unique value, extending far beyond the classroom.

The connection I built with my students wasn't limited to just knowing their names. Through laboratory classes and semester projects, I nurtured relationships, fostering mutual understanding and trust. I wanted my students to feel genuinely cared for, not just taught. This was my way of loving my neighbor as I love myself—recognizing their potential, valuing their contributions, and walking alongside them in their educational journey.

Self-love is not mere indulgence or self-centeredness; it is the foundation that enables us to fulfill the greatest commandments: to love God and love others. It begins with recognizing our intrinsic value and treating ourselves with the care and respect this understanding demands. When we acknowledge our worth, we create space within ourselves from which all meaningful relationships and acts of service can flow. Caring for my physical appearance goes beyond vanity; it reflects the respect I hold for the body I have been given. Good hygiene, dressing appropriately, and presenting myself well are not acts of superficial concern but gestures of self-respect and dignity. By honoring my body, I honor the Creator who made me, and in doing so, I am better equipped to love others as well.

In conclusion, loving God, others, and yourself are deeply interconnected—each enriching and empowering the others to create a life of purpose, peace, and profound connection. When we wholeheartedly embrace all three, we unlock a life of boundless joy, continuous growth, and a deep sense of belonging, proving that life's most meaningful chapters can still unfold after seventy-five. So, I urge you to step boldly into this truth, living each day with love as your compass. May my blessings inspire and sustain you, and may your journey be marked by the abundant and everlasting fruit of love.

A cunning fox disguises itself as holy to prey among the sheep.